to go to if you need help with anything. She is always up for the challenge. I'm pretty sure there is nothing she can't do. 2-mama is the most amazing grandparent ever!"

—AEVIN HOWARD

"2-mama is *by far* the best grandma ever! She does so much for everyone without even being asked. There isn't a task that she won't take on. She is always there for every event, recital, and ball game. There is nobody like her!"

—ASLYN HOWARD

"2-mama is *the best* at being a grandparent. She welcomes everyone, is always going out of her way to make others happy, and is always ready to have fun!"

—ASA HOWARD

"2-mama is probably the number one encourager in my life. She's always been able to help me with any of my problems. And when we leave her house, she always tells each of us, "Be a great leader and a great example."

—WILL ROBERTSON

"2-mama is the best grandma because she's involved. She wants to know how you are, how your boyfriend's doing, and how your friends are. And she's the one you want to tell it to. She is the definition of a rockstar grandma, and I love her to death."

—BELLA ROBERTSON

"2 mama is the best because she puts her children and grandkids before herself. She loves with unconditional and selfless love. And she is the biggest cheerleader for us all!"

—REBECCA LOFLIN

"2-mama is the most incredible grandma in the whole world and also one of the closest people to me. She's been there with me, and for me, through every part of my life to champion and cheer me on—from the gym for a basketball game to LA for *Dancing with the Stars*. She loves deeply, cheers loudly, and makes sure everyone is invited. I'm so thankful for who she is."

—SADIE ROBERTSON

"2-mama has been one of my most influential teachers in my life. She has taught me everything from schoolwork to party planning. Now that I am older, she has become one of my best friends, coworkers, and tennis partners."

—JOHN LUKE ROBERTSON

"2-mama really is a rockstar of a grandparent. I am married to John Luke, her oldest grandson, but she has always made me feel part of the family and so special. She has such a gift of loving people. She's the kind of grandmother you dream of and hope to be just like one day."

—MARY KATE ROBERTSON

"2-mama is the perfect example of a grandma loving her grandkids unconditionally. She serves us with a selfless heart, and she has always taught us to be the best possible version of ourselves. She supports our dreams, and she always cheers us on. 2-mama has set up a beautiful foundation for us, and I cannot thank her enough for that. I love you, 2-mama."

—MACY MOORE

"2-mama is an amazing grandma because she cares for all of us so much and always makes sure that we are taken care of before she takes care of herself. She comes to our sports games, any other extracurricular things, and everything in between. She is a wonderful grandmother!"

—ALLY MOORE

"2-mama is the best grandma because she is always encouraging us and pushing us to get out of our comfort zones to make us better. She has such a big heart and always wants to see us succeed and grow to be the best people we can be."

—MADDOX MOORE

"2-mama encourages me to strive to be as good as I can be, and she puts so much into our lives with fun surprises. Thank you, 2-mama."

—ROWDY ROBERTSON

Praise for
Rockstar Grandparent

"The influence of grandparents in the lives of their 'grands' is largely a matter of what they make of the opportunity to be steady sources of godly wisdom and counsel. Somewhat ironically, the more seriously they take the responsibility, the more fun they will have! This message is at the heart of Chrys Howard's inspiring book."

—JOHN ROSEMOND, author of *Parenting by The Book* and
other parenting bestsellers

"I've personally benefited from watching Chrys Howard juggle a crazy schedule and also grandmother her large family with grace and wisdom. Now you can score those same grandparenting 'hacks' in *Rockstar Grandparent*! Her valuable insight on handing down a legacy of faith leaves me hoping this book finds its way into the hands of grandparents far and wide."

—SHELLIE RUSHING TOMLINSON, author of *Devotions for
the Hungry Heart*

"I've read most every book on the topic of grandparenting, and *Rockstar Grandparent* stands out from the crowd. I felt as though I was in an intimate conversation with a very wise, experienced, and special friend. Chrys Howard's insights, creativity, humor, humility, powers of observation, and storytelling will delight all readers. As she delivers an abundance of wisdom and inspiration on a myriad of challenging family topics, she lavishes the reader with her deep abiding love of family and God."

—CHRISTINE CROSBY, editorial director for *Grand* magazine

"Whether you are just beginning this adventure or you consider yourself a pro, this book is full of practical advice. I am confident *Rockstar Grandparent* will equip you with the tools you need to lead your family on the journey to success."

—JOE WHITE, president of Kanakuk Kamps

"Chrys Howard had me laughing, crying, and above all, inspired to take my grandparenting to a whole new level. Not only is *Rockstar Grandparent* filled with practical and fun ideas, but it also tackles the challenges of grandparenting today and leaves the reader spiritually motivated to play a meaningful role in the lives of his or her grandchildren."

—CINDY LAMBERT, coauthor of *Unplanned*

"Ever wondered how to make a lasting difference in the lives of your grandchildren? If you long to build joy, significance, creativity, and spiritual encouragement into the young lives you mold, *Rockstar Grandparent* is for you!"

—CAROL KENT, speaker and author of *He Holds My Hand*

"Chrys gives practical ways to be a fun grandparent and shares the importance of being a united family, cheering on one another. She gives down-to-earth wisdom on how to be a positive influence in your grandchildren's lives and how to guide them to have an eternal impact on God's kingdom."

—MAC AND MARY OWEN, national directors of Celebrate Recovery

"*Rockstar Grandparent* provides the inspiration and encouragement we need to help us shine as grandparents. In her fun and whimsical way, Chrys Howard gives us practical and wise advice to creatively engage with our grandkids and make a positive difference for generations to come."

—KAROL LADD, best-selling author of *The Power of a Positive Mom*

"Think being a grandparent is a secondary role in a child's development? Think again! Chrys Howard reveals how crucial your role is and how powerfully you influence the lives of your grandkids. If you want to demonstrate your love in the best way, consider this book your guidebook."

—JOE BEAM, PhD, chair at MarriageHelper.com

"This fun book gives rock solid, rockstar advice on how to instill godly qualities in your grandchildren. Packed with plenty of great ideas, tips, and funny stories about Chrys's own grandchildren, this book is so good that you'll want to buy one for yourself and for every grandparent you know!"

—MARTHA BOLTON, author and playwright for Blue Gate Musicals

"Mom and Dad are 'the law,' but grandparents are 'the grace'—and that's what Chrys is giving us in *Rockstar Grandparent*! So spend some of your kids' inheritance and buy it!"

—DENNIS SWANBERG, "America's Minister of Encouragement"

FOREWORD BY KORIE ROBERTSON

Rockstar GRANDPARENT

How You Can
Lead the Way,
Light the Road, &
Launch a Legacy

CHRYS HOWARD

WATERBROOK

ROCKSTAR GRANDPARENT

Trade Paperback ISBN 978-0-7352-9159-1
eBook ISBN 978-0-7352-9160-7

Cover design by Mark D. Ford
Cover photo by MECKY / Getty Images; Mark D. Ford

Published in the United States by WaterBrook, an imprint of the Crown Publishing Group, a division of Penguin Random House LLC, New York.

WATERBROOK® and its deer colophon are registered trademarks of Penguin Random House LLC.

Library of Congress Cataloging-in-Publication Data
Names: Howard, Chrys, 1953- author.
Title: Rockstar grandparent : how you can lead the way, light the road, and launch a legacy / Chrys Howard.
Description: First edition. | Colorado Springs, CO : WaterBrook, 2019. | Includes bibliographical references.
Identifiers: LCCN 2018026826| ISBN 9780735291591 (pbk.) | ISBN 9780735291607 (ebook)
Subjects: LCSH: Grandparents—Religious life. | Parenting—Religious aspects—Christianity. | Child rearing—Religious aspects—Christianity.
Classification: LCC BV4528.5 .H6925 2019 | DDC 248.8/45—dc23
LC record available at https://lccn.loc.gov/2018026826

Printed in the United States of America
2019—First Edition

10 9 8 7 6 5 4 3 2 1

Dedicated to the ones we love:
Rebecca, John Luke, Sadie, Chase, Macy, Asa, Ally, Will, Maddox, Aslyn, Bella, Rowdy, Aevin, and Riley

Thank you for reintroducing us to the joyous sound of a ukulele and piano, for helping us put the latest apps on our phones, for teaching us how to properly take a selfie (and the importance of lighting), for showing us what biblical journaling is, and for coaching us on the delicacies of Raising Cane's and Chick-fil-A.

When we started our grandparenting journey, most of these things were not a thing at all. But because of you, we are challenged to see the world with new eyes and embrace the activities that define your generation, as well as instill in you an appreciation of ours. Our prayer is that we leave you a world that is better than we found it, a legacy that is full of unconditional love, and a faith that will carry you through the ups and downs that come with a life well lived.

You are loved more than you know and prayed for as much as you deserve.

Much love,
2-mama and 2-papa

Contents

Foreword

Back in the early days of Duck Commander, well before *Duck Dynasty* was even a glimmer in a Hollywood producer's eye, Willie and I began going to Las Vegas every January for the big outdoor industry trade show. We would help set up the booth and, along with the rest of the family, stand there and hope people came by to buy our family's duck calls. This trip was more than just a work trip for us, though. We'd leave the kids with their grandparents (our family calls them 2-mama and 2-papa) for the week and head to Vegas, baby. For young parents, this was an extended date we looked forward to every year!

One year I'll never forget: Our daughter Bella, who was just a little over a year old, came down with a stomach virus the night before we were to leave on the trip. *Why does it always seem to happen like that!* I remember feeling bad for her and, I have to admit, a little bit sad for myself that I wouldn't get to go on the trip. But 2-mama came over, picked her up, and said reassuringly, "You go ahead—she'll be fine." And I went. Sure enough, Bella was over the sickness in a day or two and wasn't scarred for life that I had left her. Because she had a rockstar grandma loving and caring for her, she was more than fine! Another year, both John Luke and Bella were diagnosed with the flu just days before the trip, and again 2-mama said, "Go. They'll be fine." And I went, and again they all survived.

My mom's amazing like that; not only was she the kind of grandparent who could take on sick children like it was no big deal, but she also gave me the priceless encouragement, assurance, and confidence that my kids were going to turn out all right and that I was doing a good job as a mom. I know that she loves to be with her grandkids, but taking care of sick babies isn't the most fun thing for anyone. Somehow she made it seem as if it was and allowed me to take special trips with Willie that helped strengthen our marriage and led to a little television show that a lot of people seemed to like. It was on one of those trips to Vegas that the idea for *Duck Dynasty* was born.

———

There isn't a one-size-fits-all approach to being a rockstar grandparent. For example, 2-mama is not the typical bun-in-her-hair, flour-on-her-apron grandma. She's the kind who's always up for a tennis match (you'd better bring your A game or she'll take you down) and the kind all your friends want to hang out with at her house. She throws the best parties and is the glue that holds our family together because she makes sure to celebrate the birthdays and little accomplishments of those she loves.

One of the things that makes 2-mama a rockstar is how she delights in each of her grandkids. They love for her to watch them do their thing, and she has a special way of bringing out the best in them. Ask any of her grandkids and they will tell you that 2-mama's last words as they leave her house are always "Be a good example." They take this advice seriously, and they live that way, in large part because of the example she has set for them.

Not only does 2-mama show her grandkids how to follow God

with all their hearts, how to love their neighbor, and how to live life to its fullest, but she also teaches them the little things—you know, those things that result in an eye roll when a parent says them. Things like "Sit up straight," "Chew with your mouth closed," and "Put your napkin in your lap." When 2-mama says those things, the grandkids actually seem to appreciate it. A rockstar grandparent has magic like that.

I've watched 2-mama get back out of bed at midnight when a teenage grandkid comes over for help with geometry. I've seen her on her hands and knees cleaning up every kind of mess or spill you can imagine, driving seven hours one way for a volleyball game, moving to Los Angeles for three months during *Dancing with the Stars,* and holding pets she doesn't even like (she's not really a pet lover, but for her grandkids, she can pretend with the best of them).

I plan on being that kind of grandma, and I've actually got some exciting news. Willie and I just found out we are going to be grandparents soon! Rebecca and her husband, John Reed, are expecting! My mom first taught me everything I know about being a woman of God, a kind friend, a faithful wife, a loving mom. And now I get to learn from her how to be a rockstar grandma.

I have been watching all along. I hope to have the kind of relationship with my grandkids that she has with my kids. The kind where they know my door is always open, where they can count on me to be their biggest cheerleader, where they can tell me anything, where, when tough times come, they will always have full confidence in my love for them. I'm definitely taking notes.

Our son John Luke was the first grandchild in the family. He had the honor of bestowing on Mom the name 2-mama (I'm sure she'll tell you that story later in the book; it's one of her favorites, and mine too). It fits her perfectly. I don't know how I would have raised our kiddos without her! She's a rockstar grandma in every sense of the term.

After reading her words of wisdom, you will be too.

—Korie Robertson

Introduction

*I*f you have picked up this book, *congratulations!* Either you're a new grandparent, you're about to become one, or you've been one for a while and you're having so much fun you want to learn more. Trust me—you are in one of the most exciting times of your life. Well, once you get past the fact that you're now old enough to be a grandma or grandpa, *then* the excitement can set in. Chances are you are a part of the baby boomer generation, like I am. If you came along a little later, know this about the folks a few years older than you: we have reluctantly gotten older, and at fifty, sixty, or seventy years of age, we look in the mirror each day and wonder how we turned into our parents, or we look at our peers and wonder how they got so old. Surely we're not that old!

Because I am smack-dab in the middle of the boomers, I will often refer to my generation in this book, but don't let it stop you from reading if you're not one of us. You are close enough if you have grandchildren—plus, there's a lot to learn from our far-out and groovy generation. We, the baby boomers, were born between the years of 1946 and 1964. My youngest sister was born on the same day the

Beatles made their American debut on *The Ed Sullivan Show*. That date was February 9, 1964, which makes her one of the youngest in this boomer generation. It's hard to believe, but that one show set a record with seventy-three million viewers.[1] Seventy-three million! What could a television network possibly do to get seventy-three million viewers? Well, back in those days, they didn't have to do much. We had only three channels. Remember that? With only three choices, odds were in a network's favor that they were going to get plenty of viewers. Still, no one expected the Beatles to draw a crowd of that magnitude.

Sadly, I was not one of those seventy-three million viewers. Nope, I am forever aware that I missed one of the single most iconic events in American history because my family was busy welcoming baby boomer number six. It was on February 10 that I realized how deprived I had been. I got on the school bus, eager to share news of our precious new bundle of joy, only to be met with excited screams and squeals about the "Beagles." That's exactly what my little ten-year-old ears heard. Apparently a new rock band named the "Beagles" had exploded onto the American music scene, stealing my thunder of having a new sibling. Oh well, it didn't take long for me to get the name straight and join the rest of the world singing "I Want to Hold Your Hand" and screaming for the Beatles.

While my little sister is among the last of the baby boomer generation, Phil Robertson, my co-grandparent and star of the reality show *Duck Dynasty*, was born in 1946, making him one of the first in the generation. It's been interesting to watch this eighteen-year span through the lives of my little sister and Phil Robertson. The eighteen-year difference makes baby boomers very diverse. In fact, if you were to read the facts surrounding Phil's birth and that of my little sister, you would think these two people couldn't possibly be from the same generation, but they are. Here are a few more facts.

The label *baby boomer* was given because so many babies were born during the economic boom following World War II. Historian Landon Jones described the trend by saying that almost exactly nine months after World War II ended, "the cry of the baby was heard across the land."[2] In fact, more babies were born in 1946 than ever before. And so began the baby boom. The boom finally tapered off after 1964 but not before leaving around seventy-six million[3] of us to make our mark on American history.

Along with the *baby boomer* label, we've been dubbed the TV generation, the rock-and-roll generation, and the buy-it-now-and-use-credit generation. Yes, yes, and *yes!* We are guilty of being the first generation to sit too close to a new invention called television. Our moms were happy to put us in front of shows like *The Mickey Mouse Club* and *Captain Kangaroo,* so we happily obliged them, thus becoming the first generation to be influenced by the media. And yes, we're guilty of listening to rock and roll on our transistor radios and giant stereo systems in our living rooms or blasting out our neighbors from our car radios. This led to other firsts, such as great dances like the Jerk, the Mashed Potato, and the Frug. (The Frug? Seriously?) Okay, I'm not so sure the dances were that great. Maybe we should have stuck to the classics, which would have made our parents happy, but that was not the goal of this generation. We were determined to be different. The beehive hairdo was out, and long and straight hair was in. The mellow music of Frank Sinatra was a thing of the past. We wanted it loud, or if it was soft, we wanted it full of deep meaning. And about those credit cards—we certainly are guilty of using and abusing that luxury. But hey, it sounded like a good idea at the time, right?

But we're not a lost cause by any means. Here's one description I read about us that I love. Apparently we're the first generation to use the word *retirement* to mean "get going" instead of "slow down." In other words, our generation is up and moving in ways past generations were not at our age. We're more likely to go skydiving or join a tennis league or travel the country than sit in a rocking chair. In fact, a study from Bankers Life found that "41% of baby boomers still in the workplace expect to work beyond age 69—or never retire." This same study revealed that of the baby boomers who are still working, six out of ten work because they want to. Some of the reasons cited were to stay mentally sharp, to be physically active, and to have a sense of purpose.[4] Yep, that's us.

What is wrong with us boomers? you might be asking yourself. *Why can't we just sit back and relax and leave things to the next generation?* I can't answer that question for you, but I can for myself. I just don't feel as if I'm done yet. There's more to see and more to accomplish, and with each day, my time to see and do is drawing to an end. The fact that our generation wants more for ourselves, physically and mentally, means we are increasing our chances of living longer, and that gives us more time to do the things we love. Still, we're very aware of the brevity of our lives on this earth. We might wear skinny jeans, text, work out, or ride a motorcycle, but we know we're not young anymore. Our bodies ache, and it takes us longer to text than a four-year-old, but we're not done yet. We still feel the need to be significant members of modern society.

So, grandparents, you might still be playing in a band like Paul McCartney or competing in tennis tournaments like Chris Evert, or you might be a strong player in the workforce like Warren Buffett, but now you also hold one of the most important titles you will ever hold, and that's Grandma or Grandpa.

According to the website Grandparents.com, 1.7 million new grandparents are added every year with an overall number of 70 million grandparents in the States today.[5] Wow! And from the posts you put on Facebook, it's clear you think you're the *only* grandparents in America! I'm just kidding. Keep posting those grandkid pics. I'm going to. It's part of who we are. That same website says that 75 percent of us are online users. There's no grass growing under our feet. We're going to figure out how to stay connected, aren't we? Even if we have to get our grandkids to connect us and tell us for the tenth time how to use Twitter! (Yes, true confessions from this social media grandma.)

So here we are. We may not look or act like grandparents of the past, but we are the grandparents for this newest generation. As I said earlier, you might be a grandparent to a newborn, or like me, you may have a grandchild in his or her twenties (how did this happen?). In any case, this is the generation we are charged with affecting. A generation that hasn't been officially dubbed anything. A generation that faces challenges we didn't even know could exist. So the question is, How can we accomplish this? As connected as we try to be, relating to this "wired" generation will be challenging.

This younger generation will never know the fun of snuggling with siblings while wearing pajamas at a drive-in movie. Many won't know what it's like to play outside until dark and hear Mom yell, "Dinner's ready!" They won't experience watching a good western like *Bonanza* with the whole family in one room. Many of our grandkids will never know the joy and trials of sharing a room with a sibling. No, this new generation has choices and options—too many, that's for sure. Too many TV shows, too many pairs of jeans, too many sports or other activities. They are a generation of excess.

Is there a place for us grandparents in their excessive world? You bet there is! Grandparents are the glue that will hold this world together. My mom is eighty-seven years old and is the reigning matriarch of our family. Until age eighty-four, she worked full time. She is on Facebook, dresses like a movie star, and attends as many grandkid and great-grandkid activities as her busy schedule allows. One day she told me her goal in her later years is to remain relevant. I told her she has achieved that goal. Born in 1931, Mom is part of what has been dubbed the silent generation. The silent generation includes babies born from 1925 to 1945. Some of the descriptors I discovered for the silent generation include *enjoy reading, love big-band music, loyal, self-sacrificing,* and *cautious.* My mom has all these traits. But she didn't follow the rocking-chair grandma mold that defines many of her peers. She spent what others consider retirement years active in work, church, and community life. She set the stage for her children as we entered our own grandparenting years. She showed us that a world of possibilities still awaits us even after our children are grown and gone. I have five siblings, and we constantly tell Mom to slow down so we can! So, baby boomers, we can't take all the credit for debunking the rocking-chair grandma mentality. My mom single-handedly took on the challenge.

One thing our generation loves to boast about is our music. We proudly declare it the best! Join me as we take a look at some of the songs that influenced our generation. Each chapter will be introduced with a song from our era. I know it's an eighteen-year span, but you'll get it. I'm sure you didn't realize that many of our generation's favorite songs addressed our grandparenting years. As you were rocking out to the top twenty hits, you weren't thinking about your life as a grandparent. And there's no doubt these artists didn't realize they were speaking about being a grandparent either, but they were. Okay, there was that one song we all sang and loved, and it really was about being old, but we couldn't imagine being *that* old. Sing it with me: "Will you still need me . . ."[6]

Good job! Seriously, that song was great, but losing our hair or knitting a sweater or anything that went along with old age was not a serious threat when we first heard that song—*yet!* Those things were so far in the future that we laughed about them. We're still laughing. Only now we're laughing because they all came true. I want to say thank you to all the great musical geniuses who helped our generation put our feelings into words. Those words are still influencing our lives.

Yes, this generation of long-haired, self-centered, bell-bottomed, barefoot, spaced-out, rocking teenagers has finally grown up. Hopefully we've also grown out of the negative monikers we were given and are proud to be called Grandma and Grandpa. Or is it Nana and Papa? Or Honey and Pa? Or Mimi and Pops? Or Gigi and Big Daddy? Here we go again, being our rebellious selves! Did anyone seriously think we would be happy with the titles Grandma and Grandpa? Nope. Not us. We're way too young for those names!

I realize that I've said a lot about baby boomers and that the premise of the book rests on baby boomer songs, but I'm aware that many grandparents are a few years short of being a boomer or may have been born a little before this generation. Don't let that stop you from reading this book. It's full of hints, tips, and advice that are good for grandparents all of ages and in all stages.

So, Nana and Papa or Honey and Pa or Mimi and Pops or Gigi and Big Daddy, hang loose and enjoy the world of grandparenting. Trust me—it's a far-out, neato, and groovy place to be! You're well on your way to being a rockstar grandparent to some very special children.

Hugs,

Chrys

Turn! Turn! Turn!

*T*his popular song was written by Pete Seeger in the late 1950s and made famous by a singing group called the Byrds in 1965. (The Byrds, the Beatles, the Monkees, the Who, the Kinks—good grief! What were we thinking?) As Pete Seeger explained it, he received a letter from his publisher telling him he couldn't sell Seeger's protest songs (shocker—a protest song in the '60s!) and asked him to come up with something he could sell. Seeger said he got mad (again, shocker, right?) and then wrote the melody to "Turn! Turn! Turn!" in fifteen minutes.[1] That's pretty impressive, even if the lyrics were already supplied for him.

Here's another interesting fact about that song. When you go to Wikipedia, you will notice it says music by Pete Seeger and lyrics by the book of Ecclesiastes. I know Wikipedia isn't the best source of information, but this fact is correct. The lyrics of this song are straight from Ecclesiastes. Pete Seeger, in order to produce words that were not protesting something, turned to the Bible and came up with a number one hit song.

As it turns out, the words in Ecclesiastes 3 were perfect for our generation of deep thinkers (we thought we were anyway). But the truth is, these words are perfect for every generation. In His wisdom, God knew that each generation would have to come to terms with the word *turn*. There are many definitions of this word, and like many American words, we use it in several ways. We learn to "take turns." We're asked to "turn over" something. We say "turn on" the light or TV or oven.

One definition of the word *turn* that I like for the purpose of this chapter is the following: "an opportunity or obligation to do something that comes successively to each of a number of people."[2] That seems to be the definition God was referring to when inspiring the words in Ecclesiastes. Each successive group of people, in various times of their lives, will have the opportunity to take a turn at a number of different events and activities.

Let's look at the idea of taking turns. You learned to take turns when you were somewhere around two years old. You know the scenario. Your three-year-old sibling jumped in front of you to get on the slide, and your mom calmly grabbed your sibling and said, "No, you have to take turns. It's little sister's turn now." And you happily got to go in front of that big sister or brother. All was well until you were the one held back so someone else could take a turn. Right?

Some think this is the beginning of sharing, but sharing is another concept we learn. Sharing implies that you work together; taking turns means to totally hand over the reins of something to someone else. This song is a great reminder that we have a season and that when our season is over, it will be time to turn things over to someone else.

A few years ago I traveled with my granddaughter Sadie Robertson to an appearance. While there, I ran into a sweet young lady who, at one point, attended a church in our city and knew our family. She had a troubled life as a child but as an adult found peace and hope in God. She asked whether she could bless me and pray over me. Of course I said yes. Her words touched my heart in a profound way. She said that the hard work my husband and I had done in the kingdom, the plowing and tilling, would be the foundation for our children and grandchildren to serve God. Then she said, "Your ceiling will be the floor for the lives of your grandchildren." Wow! All the things we worked for, prayed about, achieved, aimed at, conquered, cried over, and fought for are laid down as the floor for our grandchildren to build on! I have thought about this, and its implications for life, over and over. The picture became very clear on a special trip we took.

For Christmas in 2017, my husband, Johnny, and I decided to take our entire family to Israel for a tour of the Holy Land. (I'll refer to this trip a few more times in this book because the experience was like no other. If it's not on your bucket list, add it . . . right now!) It was such a blessing to walk with my kids and grandkids where Jesus walked; it's something they will never forget. One of the most interesting things we witnessed was how civilizations were built on top of one another. Through years of excavating, layers of different civilizations have been discovered. In other words, one civilization's ceiling became the floor of another civilization. I was able to see a physical example of what that sweet lady was telling me about the legacy Johnny and I were leaving to our grandchildren.

As each generation (or civilization) works and toils to build their lives, they are setting the stage for the next generation to build on top. There is a section in Jerusalem where we were able to look down a large hole and see the remnants of three civilizations. Talk about taking turns!

A civilization was built on top of another until centuries came and went, leaving the new civilization no clues of what lay beneath them.

Isn't this true of our lives? I have no idea what specific things my great-grandparents did on a day-to-day basis, but I do know—because it has been handed down to me—that they loved God. I'm fairly confident they didn't attend anything that resembled a major youth rally like Passion, which Louie and Shelley Giglio so masterfully put together. I can also say with confidence that they didn't attend a summer camp where they played games and swam in a big pool. No, these types of things didn't exist. But I'm pretty sure they attended church when the church bell chimed, they fed the hungry, they cared for the sick, they went to the church potluck, and they tucked their kids into bed at night and prayed over them.

You see, the layers of spiritual civilizations will look as different as physical civilizations do. We, as a society and as individual people, grow and change; our methods change, but our message does not. In every civilization, in every generation, the message is still to love God and love and serve others. As long as we continue to lay that foundation, it will become the floor for the lives of our children and grandchildren. Then it will be their turn to light up the world with God's message.

One other way I can see this scenario is by looking at our homesite. Our family home is located on an old homestead. When we built our house, we found markings that let us know another family at one point lived on our land. I love to walk under our huge oak tree and think about the other families that took their turn living on this property. I imagine someone else's children running in the field and horses or cows grazing in the pasture. But today it's our turn for this property. Our house sits pretty close to where we imagine the original home sat, but it's air-conditioned and much larger than that home. We have a barn, possibly like our predecessors, but ours is home to workout equipment instead of hay and farm equipment. We have two cars that come and go daily on a concrete driveway that took the place of the dirt drive they would have traveled on. There's a swing set and a volleyball net set up for the grandkids to enjoy. During our turn we hope we are making it better for the next family to take their turn. Making things better should always be our goal as we use the resources God gives us.

But there are always two questions to answer when it's time to take turns. First, am I ready or willing to allow another to take his turn, and second, what if there's no one to take over after me? Those are two very good questions. In fact, even at two years old when we are first confronted with taking turns, we have to decide whether we are going to obey our parents and let the other child have a turn or whether we are going to rebel and jump on that slide before the other child gets there. Hopefully, with some prodding, we all come to the right conclusion that taking turns is beneficial for everyone.

Taking turns establishes in us the ability to let go of ourselves and let others take priority. Isn't that the true nature of Christianity—laying aside our desires for the desires of another? Philippians 2:3 tells us to "do nothing out of selfish ambition" (NIV). The New Living Translation says it this way: "Don't be selfish; don't try to impress others. Be humble, thinking of others as better than yourselves." The very act of Jesus dying on the cross for us is proof that God values others over Himself. That was, of course, the ultimate sacrifice.

Remember the little JOY acronym? Jesus first, others second, and yourself third. You probably learned that in Sunday school when you didn't want that superfast kid in your fourth-grade class to get to the water fountain first. Perhaps your teacher lectured the class with the JOY acronym. Still, it wasn't easy. Putting others first is a lifelong battle with our flesh. It seems life would be easier if everyone would do everything the way I want things done. Right? Yes, but that's wrong. As we grow and mature in the Lord, we finally understand that putting others first actually gives us a better version of self-satisfaction. Letting others have a turn takes maturity to another level because no one likes to give up what feels good and comfortable.

On to question number two—what if there's no one to take over after me? Or what if she can't do it as well as I have done it? What if she messes everything up that I worked so hard to achieve? What if she *doesn't* leave the world a better place? The what-ifs could drive you crazy, but they're totally contrary to what the song "Turn! Turn! Turn!" and the Bible tell us. God designed us for a specific time and place. Our finite minds can barely fathom God's plan and how He manages the entire earth and the bazillion people who have occupied it. I had three kids who kept me hopping like a frog on a steamy Friday night trying to get away from the likes of frog hunter Jason Robertson. Now I have those three kids, their spouses, and fourteen grandkids to keep up with. It's enough to make me want to holler uncle. My calendar looks as if I'm the president of the United States or the head of a major corporation instead of a busy grandma. How does God do it? How does He manage the sun, the moon, the stars, and millions of people? Because He's God, that's how. It's what He does. And we don't even have to worry about it.

Like it or not, your turn as a parent is over and your kids are now in charge. I know that it can be a scary thought. My daddy was a wise man, and he always told me no one was irreplaceable. In our lifetime, we have seen amazing men and women come and go. Remarkable, brilliant minds like Steve Jobs; unforgettable acting talents like John Wayne; funny men like John Ritter and Robin Williams; amazing voices like Whitney Houston; and on and on. All these men and women held a big enough place in this world that many wondered who would replace them. And then someone did. Their turns were over. New voices, new ideas, new jokes—something new replaces what we thought was irreplaceable. This is God's design.

In a five-year span, my husband and I lost three of our parents. My dad and both of my husband's parents have now gone on to their heavenly home. There was a time when I couldn't imagine living without a parent. You might have felt the same way before you lost your parents. Perhaps, like me, you have woken up many mornings thinking you need to call Mom or Dad, but Mom or Dad isn't there anymore. That's when you realize his or her turn is over. Now it's your turn. Nothing more clearly defines a turn than for someone to be gone completely.

Yes, "to everything there is a season." We will each take our turn at being a child, a teenager, a mom or dad, and then a grandparent. It's the circle of life that is so beautifully displayed in the movie and play *The Lion King*. We took our grandkids to the musical production on Broadway. It made me want to hold one of them up in the air and shout for joy. Sadly, most of mine outweigh me now, making that impossible, but you get the point. Handing down the legacy of your family to the next generation is one of life's most glorious callings.

Consider again the words of the song. Right after "To everything there is a season" comes this phrase: "and a time to every purpose under heaven." Finding our purpose. "Whoa! That's heavy," as we used to say in the '60s. For many, reaching this stage in life brings confusion and uncertainty about their purpose. Many have invested so much in their old lives that a new one feels not only unfamiliar but also unwanted. To add to the confusion, words like *baby wipe warmers* make you wonder how you ever raised your own kids.

My grandpa loved puzzles. I can still see him sitting in front of a one-thousand-piece puzzle, studying the front of the box, memorizing what the puzzle should look like when he finished it. He told me the secret to putting together a puzzle is to find the corners first, then work on the straight edges. Once the corners were in place and the borders secure, I could start on the inside. He didn't know it, or maybe he did, but he was teaching me about life. I was learning that in order for me to put the pieces of my life together, I had to first find my corners. I had to find what mattered the most to me and lock those things in. Then I had to build from those foundations and secure the boundaries I needed that would frame up my life. That's called defining your purpose.

> ★ ★ ★ ★
> *Rockstar*
> GRANDPARENTING
>
> It's your turn to be the wise one; the experienced one; the tried, true, and tested one.

Your life is like a one-million-piece puzzle. The good—no, great—news about this stage of life is that your corners are probably pretty secure. You've raised your family, worked forever, and established yourself in your church and community. Gone are the days of wondering what you'll be when you grow up or how you'll handle the death of a loved one or the loss of a job or the betrayal of a friend. Chances are you've experienced similar scenarios in life and conquered them. But there are still a few pieces missing from your puzzle. Your puzzle needs your grandparenting years to make it complete. Like that missing piece you find under the couch, your grandparenting years are the pieces your life puzzle has been waiting for. And trust me—this part of the puzzle is the fun part. With all your boundaries firmly in place, you can now put that last piece in and glue it together.

Oh, I'm not saying there won't be surprises and disappointments. Life doesn't stop being real when you become a grandparent. You are just better equipped than you were when you became a parent. You've lived a few years and seen a few things.

Many years ago I read an essay about the end of our lives and how great it is that our grandchildren see only the end and not the beginning. I've thought of that many times as I watched my parents in their grandparenting and great-grandparenting roles. I understand the premise, for sure, and know there are things we all did in our youth that we wish we hadn't, but still, it would have been fun for my children to see my parents when they were young and vibrant. John Luke would have played racquetball with my dad, and the girls would have bowled or played tennis with my mom. That would have been fun. But as much as I love fun, life isn't all about the fun things. It's about the fruitful things—the things that are intangible.

It's funny how, by definition, intangible things are things we cannot hold or grasp, yet it's the intangibles we hold on to with the firmest grip. When it was time for my parents to stop playing racquetball and hang out in the bowling alley, they never stopped the most important things in life, such as being kind, loving unconditionally, and whispering prayers of hope, peace, and joy.

In your grandparenting role, you are no less important than you have been at any time in your life. It's just a new time. It's time to look at what you've accomplished and see what your next step is. It's your turn to be the wise one; the experienced one; the tried, true, and tested one; and the one who can pass that wisdom, experience, and tested-ness (okay, maybe not a real word, but you get it) on to the next generation. Our future generations depend on you and me! There's much to teach them. After all, without us, who would show them how to play marbles, belt out "Hey Jude," and tell a Laffy Taffy joke?

═══════

There is a time for everything,
    and a season for every activity under the heavens:
    a time to be born and a time to die,
    a time to plant and a time to uproot,
    a time to kill and a time to heal,
    a time to tear down and a time to build,
    a time to weep and a time to laugh,
    a time to mourn and a time to dance,
    a time to scatter stones and a time to gather them,
    a time to embrace and a time to refrain from
        embracing,
    a time to search and a time to give up,
    a time to keep and a time to throw away,
    a time to tear and a time to mend,
    a time to be silent and a time to speak,
    a time to love and a time to hate,
    a time for war and a time for peace.

—ECCLESIASTES 3:1–8, NIV

The Name Game

I want you to raise your hand if you were on a road trip, or maybe on a school bus, when an impromptu performance of this silly song broke out:

> Grandma! Grandma, Grandma bo-band-ma
> Bo-na-na, fanna fo-fand-ma
> Fee fi mo-mand-ma, Grandma!

I'll go ahead and admit it: this little ditty helped pass the time for many a family on vacation when cars didn't have TVs and kids didn't have smartphones. While it was written by Shirley Ellis and released in 1964, it's gone on to have a long and fruitful life. It appeared in a Little Caesars pizza commercial in 1993, and Tom Hanks sang it in the 1986 movie *The Money Pit* while he waited to be rescued from a fall through the ceiling. The words and tune seem to cross all boundaries of logic and lyrics. It's just plain fun. If you haven't done it in a while (or ever), wait until there's a quiet moment and belt it out using one of your grandkid's names. The kids are sure to look up from their technology when they hear you singing something like this: "Sadie, Sadie bo-ba-die . . ."

The name of the song is "The Name Game." That makes sense, doesn't it? It's just taking anyone's name and playing a fun lyrical game with it. I think our generation has been playing its own version of the name game. Choosing our grandma and grandpa names has become a fun and vital part of today's grandparenting journey. I'm waiting for someone to start the "grandma/grandpa name reveal party" tradition. I can see it now. Grandma and Grandpa have a ribbon with letters on it stretched between them with their new names dangling for everyone to ooh and ah over. Maybe a little over the top, you say? But did we even consider a gender-reveal party, held before the baby shower, just after the wedding shower, which came after the engagement party, which came after the . . . you get the picture. Times have changed. It's a world of celebrating and documenting all of it on social media.

Whoops, I got off track! Back to the grandparents' name game. There was a time when everyone called grandparents the same thing or a slight variation of the same thing. I can remember hearing Grandma and Grandpa, Papaw and Mamaw, and Granny and Pa, but that was about it. When I was growing up, I had Grandma and Grandpa Shack and Grandma and Grandpa Durham. That's it. My kids added Papaw Shack and Mamaw Jo and Papaw and Mamaw Howard, plus their great-grandparents I already mentioned, but all the names were similar.

Any way you look at it, apparently people weren't as creative in those years as we are today. I'm inclined to believe there is more to the story than our creativity, and it might go back to our rebellious roots.

When we, the boomers, reached the grandparenting age, we didn't look, act, or feel as if we should be there, and names like Granny and Pa were not going to cut it. Am I right? In fact, I can remember my son-in-law Willie Robertson saying he just couldn't call me Grandma or Mamaw. I was good with that. I couldn't see myself being called those names either. But what would they call me?

I read recently that one of the things that separate the human race from the animal kingdom is the ability to use language. Of course, I knew this to be true, but I hadn't thought about it in terms of the names we give one another. We name dogs, but they don't name us. And I have yet to hear one dog call another by the name we have given him. Putting together letters to become words that become a means of identifying each person is a highly intelligent level of communication, but it's one that comes easily to us humans. Still, picking a name for your child can be one of the most brain-taxing, argument-inducing, family-dividing, research-spurring events connected with the new bundle of joy. When Sadie was born, Korie decided her middle name would be Carroway, which is Willie's mother's, Miss Kay's, maiden name. I shuddered thinking of our little baby Sadie having such a big name. Now I can't imagine her being named anything but Sadie Carroway. Names grow on us, don't they?

Just as your little babies grew into the names you chose for them, you will grow into your grandparenting name. Whatever your firstborn grandchild calls you will be the best name ever in the history of names! "So . . . be your name Buxbaum or Bixby or Bray or Mordecai Ali Van Allen O'Shea," as the Dr. Seuss book says, "you're off to Great Places!"[1] Because no matter what your grandkids call you, you will answer. My grandkids call me 2-mama, which I love. And they call Johnny 2-papa. Here's our grandparenting name story.

When my first grandchild, John Luke, was born, his grandma on the other side was already an established grandma with the now-famous (because of *Duck Dynasty*) name Mamaw Kay. Three of his great-grandmothers were still alive, which meant he had Mamaw Jo, Mamaw Howard, and Granny Robertson. It made perfect sense for me to be Mamaw Chrys. *Hold the phone!* We just established that I wouldn't be a Mamaw, didn't we? Of course we did! Here's what happened. Much to my joy, when John Luke started talking, he called his mom (Korie) Mama, *and* he called me Mama. As honored as I was to have this name, I knew it wasn't sustainable. (It's confusing just explaining it to you.) We seriously tried every grandma name we could think of, but nothing worked. My nieces and nephews call me Chryssy, so we tried Kissy (cute, huh?) and Mama Chryssy and CC. Out of desperation, we even tried Mamaw Chrys. Nope. (Praise the Lord!) Mama was his name for both of us, which was very confusing to all parties involved. Then Korie was put on bed rest in the last few months of her pregnancy with Sadie, leaving John Luke to spend hours with me (I loved it!). The Mama name seemed to be sticking. However, I determined it wasn't a good thing (at least, I said that to others), and I always corrected him and said Korie was his mama.

A few weeks after Sadie was born, I was keeping John Luke for the day. When it was time to return my precious firstborn grandchild to his mother, he didn't want to go. (BTW, grandmas, isn't that the best?) He was crying and calling me Mama, and I was telling him Korie was his mama—and back and forth we went. Then, out of nowhere, he looked at me and called me 2-mama. I'm pretty sure a chorus of hallelujahs rang out far and wide, because this was the perfect grandma name.

Now, there are a couple of theories floating around as to how John Luke came up with this name. I forgot to mention he was only twenty-one months old. (I know—he was brilliant, wasn't he? Remember, I said naming is a highly intelligent gift.) The first theory is the one my husband stands by, but I'll just tell you right up front, grandpas are not as attuned to their grandkids as grandmas are. However, I let him have his say. He says John Luke heard Korie referring to me when she spoke to Willie in this way: "Let's go over *to* Mama's house for dinner." Or "I'm going *to* Mama's house for a minute." Thus, John Luke heard the words *to* and *Mama* together and decided it was my name. I admit, that in itself makes him a pretty smart kid. But I have another theory, and I'm sure it's the right one.

As I said, our newest grandbaby, Sadie, had just arrived. I found myself saying, "We have two babies now." My theory is John Luke said to himself, *How cool is this? I must have two mamas. One I'll call Mama and the other one (the one I love so much) I'll call 2-mama.* Of course, he didn't verbalize any of that; it was just said in his head. Now, at twenty-two, he can't remember any of it, rendering him no help at all. In any case, I have happily been called 2-mama for nearly twenty-two years, and my husband is called 2-papa. There was a brief possibility of another name when Sadie reached talking age, because she struggled with the *t* sound and couldn't get out "2-mama." She started calling me Kissy (remember, the nieces and nephews call me Chryssy), and I loved that too, but John Luke won that battle, and 2-mama still stands today.

When I'm with my friends who are now grandmas, I hear such fun names. Honey, Mimi, GiGi, J-mama, Bec, Mim, and Nonnie are just a few. Grandpas have gotten pretty creative too these days. I hear Pa, Big Daddy, Papa T, Pap, and even Grumpy. It can be fun to choose a name that fits your personality or, as we did with John Luke, let the children come up with the name—or at least the first grandchild. After the first one, it's usually a done deal. Many times in a child's innocent mispronunciation of a name, a good grandma name is born. That's how my friend Connie became known as Nonnie to her grands.

On the practical side, it helps when you're on the playground or in a store to have a different name from other grandparents. Think about all those times you heard "Mama" when your children were growing up and everyone looked to see who was actually being called. (Still today, if I hear "Mama," I'm likely to turn and look. Keep in mind, there's not a chance in the world it's coming from one of my children, but old habits die hard!) Having my own unique grandma name means when I hear "2-mama," I have no doubt one of my grands is looking for me. As you would expect, Hollywood has embraced the name game with names like Honey for Susan Sarandon, GoGo for Goldie Hawn, and Lalo for Blythe Danner. All good grandma names for sure, but I still contend mine is the best.

But there's a downside to this new trend. I will never find a shirt, coffee mug, key chain, or wall hanging with *2-mama* on it unless my grands make it themselves. I have a line of grandma T-shirts that are trendy and cute, but I can't possibly put specific grandma names on each shirt. I have come to the conclusion that a grandma by any other name is still a grandma. And the same is true for grandpas. Being grandparents is the position we hold, not necessarily the names we answer to. It's no different from children calling their dad Pops or Big Daddy. Pops or Big Daddy, in the end, is their dad.

Being a grandparent is the most delightful journey and the most gratifying role you will ever play. How sweet it is to hold the child of your child in your arms. One of my favorite quotes about grandparenting is by author and columnist Lois Wyse. She said, "Grandchildren are the dots that connect the lines from generation to generation."[2] I love that. I have another one. I say grandparents are the link in the chain of life that connects the past to the future.

When I think about the role my grandparents played in my life, I know that without them the legacy of my family would be incomplete. My grandparents on my mother's side left their home in Arkansas to find work in San Diego during World War II. My grandfather served as a civilian carpenter at the Naval Amphibious Base Coronado, and my grandmother painted instrument dials on naval aircraft at the Naval Air Station North Island. What a heritage. These hardworking Americans risked it all to support their country and provide for their family. Later in life, my grandmother, Grandma Durham, went back to school to become a nurse.

Now keep in mind, I'm old, making my grandmother a woman of great vision long before the cry of the '60s women's movement. She just did what she knew she needed to do to be a vital part of her community. My grandfather never went to church with my grandma; however, he was raised in a strong Christian family. Grandma passed on her faith to her children, which ultimately led to my mother being the strong Christian leader she is to our family. Again, long before women were being told to stand up, my grandmother stood up. She knew what she believed, and she was not going to back down.

My grandmother on my dad's side, Grandma Shack, was of Native American descent. Her Choctaw dad and French mother were second-generation survivors of the Trail of Tears, ending up in Oklahoma, where my dad was born. My grandfather had a love for alcohol, and that love won out over his love for his wife and seven children. My grandmother eventually left him and went on to support her family by working in a school cafeteria. One of her sons died at age sixteen in a motorcycle accident, which brought her deep pain. Still, she worked hard and proudly carried on as her five remaining sons served our country in wartime and later went on to college. Her only daughter also attended and graduated from college, becoming a teacher at a time when young girls rarely went to college. My grandma was only four feet eleven, but she was a little stick of dynamite. She was tenacious and witty and beat anyone who dared challenge her to a game of Scrabble.

Did my grandparents attend every sporting event we participated in? No, hardly any. Did my grandmothers cater to our every whim? Never. One Christmas I remember getting a pair of pantyhose from my Grandma Shack and thinking it was the greatest gift in the world. Did my grandfather take my brothers fishing and hunting? Nope. They weren't bad grandparents. They were awesome grandparents! I loved them dearly. But the times were different. Even though they didn't attend our sporting events or take us hunting, I learned many things from my grandparents.

From my tiny Grandma Shack I learned that we can do more than we think possible. That no job is beneath you if you love your family. I learned the history of the Choctaw Indians as she told stories handed down from her father. In her later years, she lovingly handwrote many of those stories for future generations to remember and reflect on. She was a wealth of knowledge about her Choctaw heritage, and she was intent on passing that knowledge on. I know I speak for all my cousins when I say our pride in our heritage comes from a sometimes cranky, always witty, minuscule Native American woman.

From my Grandma Durham I learned quiet perseverance. This grandma wasn't outspoken or dynamic, but she was faithful. She faithfully served her family, her church, and her community. I can still see her sitting in her chair in her living room, Bible open, determined to learn more about God's Word. The simple fact that she pursued a nursing career when others were looking toward retirement told me that our job on earth isn't over until it's over. Maybe that's why I'm writing a book at age sixty-four. There's always more to do.

My Grandpa Shack, the one who

★ ★ ★ ★
Rockstar
GRANDPARENTING

"Be your name Buxbaum or Bixby or Bray or Mordecai Ali Van Allen O'Shea," as the Dr. Seuss book says, "you're off to Great Places!" Because no matter what your grandkids call you, you will answer.

was an alcoholic, wasn't often in our lives, but my dad never failed to mention that he passed his gift of humor on to his children. Even amid my dad's disappointment in him, he looked for the good. There are no members of that generation left on my dad's side today, but I remember family reunions in which my dad and his brothers would laugh, often over the antics of their father, and entertain the family for hours. The great sense of humor I see in my siblings and cousins I'm sure comes from an Irish grandpa who couldn't shake an alcohol addiction.

My Grandpa Durham, the one who never went to church with us, revealed on his deathbed that he always believed he was one of the civilian carpenters selected to build the crate that carried the atomic bomb to Japan. He proudly served his country, and he didn't speak of this until he was ninety-two years old. He told my mother that he had been blindfolded and taken to a building site where instructions were given to him. Once the job was complete, he was again blindfolded and returned to his home, where he was sworn to secrecy. The secrecy directive was lifted many years before his death, but he chose to remain silent about it. This was just one of the times I witnessed this man of integrity hold his tongue and do the right thing. My capable, God-fearing, family-loving grandmother was diagnosed with dementia around age sixty-three. My grandfather cared for her until it was impossible for him to manage alone, and they moved in with my mom and dad.

I'm sharing all this to say, again, to all you grandparents out there, you have the greatest job ever! You are the link to the past that your grandchildren need in their lives. The past is what gives our present and future a sense of security and purpose. Although my grandparents didn't attend every event their grandchildren participated in, I never doubted their love for me. How do I know they loved me? That's a good question too. I seriously can't remember them telling me they loved me. They just did. I could see it in their eyes and feel it in their hugs and taste it in their homemade biscuits, and I could save it in the little wooden box Grandpa Durham made for me that still holds doll clothes for my grandchildren.

The world has changed significantly since I was a little girl. My experiences don't give me the same stories to tell my grandchildren. I didn't work in a cafeteria to support seven children as a single mom. I didn't serve during wartime. But I lived a life different from the ones my grandchildren are living. Every generation does. There are still stories I need to tell and a heritage I need to pass on. I can tell the stories of their Native American great-great-grandmother and show them the hand-written book I now cherish hidden high in my closet. There are many gifts we can give this generation. We'll look more deeply at them later in this book, but one gift that is unique to this generation is the gift of availability. Even if you don't live in the same town as your grands, you are still just a FaceTime call away from them. What a blessing that is. I'm sure my grandparents would have loved the gift of time with their grandchildren, but again, times were different. We have the ability today to be an active support system for our children and grandchildren. Let's take full advantage of it.

This chapter started out looking at the name our grandchildren decide to call us, but it's easy to see that being their grandparent is the sweetest job we'll have and that whatever name they call us will be the sweetest sound we'll hear!

———————

Choose a good reputation over great riches;
  being held in high esteem is better than silver
  or gold.

—Proverbs 22:1

Help! I Need Somebody—Help!

For a generation of teens who prided ourselves on self-reliance and making our own way, the fact that the Beatles sang about needing help was confusing. But like all teens, we were eager to embrace the current tone of the culture, so we joined them in singing, "Help! I need somebody!" because maybe we all *did* need help. After all, no man is an island, right?

Let's explore the "I need help" dilemma a bit. To need help requires an admission that some area of our lives is lacking. In my observation, some humans are born with an "I need help" gene, while others are born with an "I got this" gene. Think back to when your children were littles. All kiddos at around eighteen months of age learn to say "I do it." If you were like me, you were bursting with pride, even if their grammar wasn't correct. We bragged on their independent spirit. But a year or two later, the one with the "I got this" gene was driving you crazy! He wouldn't let you button his shirt, making you late to a doctor's appointment. She refused to let you fix her hair, resulting in a virtual bird's nest at the back of her head. He said no to every suggestion you thought would be the perfect shirt for school pictures. The little independent spirit you were bursting with pride over had become annoyingly stubborn. And so it went, until you handed her her hat and coat and sent her off to college, praying for her roommate.

On the flip side, you might have had one who easily accepted help. In fact, you look back and realize you carried him until he was four! When she was a toddler, you loved that this personality type treasured snuggle time with Mommy, right? Well, you loved it until you realized you couldn't breathe without said child wanting to be right beside you. The child you loved to snuggle and hug became the one you wanted to hide from, even for a minute to use the bathroom. And so it went, until you handed him his hat and coat and sent him off to college, knowing the phone would ring within minutes of his leaving.

For the most part, all children have tendencies both ways. There are times when they are independent and don't want any help, and there are times they need us as if they are two years old. In full disclosure, my personality isn't needy. I'm the one who will carry the garbage out to the trash can even if it is twice my weight or sweep the entire back porch on a one-hundred-degree summer day while six teenagers sit in my house in the air-conditioning. I know—it's ridiculous. I just don't easily ask for help. It's a fault. Over the years I've learned (but it's been hard) that others want to help and, in fact, it makes them feel good to help me. I know this is true, because I love to help others. I just have a hard time when it is reciprocated. And for the record, I'm a quiet, stubborn person too. Does that make sense? I was the child who quietly didn't ask for help, doing everything for myself. You might have one of those in your family. The one who doesn't make waves. The one who doesn't disturb the peace. The one who just does his or her own thing, quietly. That was me.

I became a married woman at eighteen, moved off to college with my new hubby, and began my life as an adult. *I got this,* I thought. After all, how hard can it be to go to school, keep a house trailer in order (we lived between the meatpacking plant and a cemetery—there's more than a few jokes going around about that), cook three meals a day, play a few sports, support my husband's activities, make my own clothes, attend church, and have a fun social life? I think it took about a week before I called my mom with the "How do I cook chicken?" question. Knowing what I know now, as a mom and grandma, I would wager that phone call was the best call my mom got that day. In that one phone call, I said to her, "You are still needed. You are valuable. I need you to help me."

As a younger me, I was guilty of thinking two things about asking for help. One, I thought asking for help might be a sign of weakness. My quiet, independent self didn't want to admit that I might not be able to conquer a particular task. I learned over the years that asking for help isn't a sign of weakness; it's a sign of love and trust. I called my mom to find out about cooking chicken because I trusted that she would do everything in her power to help me make awesome fried chicken. (Bless her heart, she did try, but I'm deficient in the amazing-cooking gene area!) I asked her for help because I knew that she loved me and that no matter what was on her calendar for the day, my phone call was top priority. She made me feel as if she wanted me to interrupt her day. (She still does. Recently I gave her a bunch of overripe bananas and she returned that same day with banana nut bread. Now, that's an amazing mom!)

The other misconception I had about asking for help, and the biggest one for me, was that by asking for help, I'd be putting someone else out. It goes like this: I don't want you to have to do what I can do, because you have your own things to do. I'm confident some of this is learned behavior. My mom is the queen of "I can do it." She begs to help us do anything we're doing, but she doesn't dare ask us to help her. Okay, we all have our issues, right? In our defense, sociologically speaking, people of our eras (Mom's and mine) just take care of their own business. It's likely you grew up in the same era. Do you remember the words your mom said as you left the house to play outside? It was probably "Don't go in anyone else's house." This is great advice and words we might use today out of fear for our children's safety, but our moms' motive wasn't the fear that fuels safety briefings; it was the fear that fuels discipline. Under no circumstances were children to mess up someone else's house. I learned early on that you don't put anyone out.

The two new generations living on the planet today are very different from the previous generations. Psychologist Jean Twenge described millennials as "Generation Me" in her 2006 book, *Generation Me: Why Today's Young Americans Are More Confident, Assertive, Entitled—and More Miserable Than Ever Before.*[1] She updated the book in 2014. There is still debate as to the years that define the millennials, but most researchers say this generation includes those born from the late 1970s to the mid-1990s. Now, folks, keep this in mind when you are critical of this "me" generation—you probably raised one or more of them!

Before you get down on yourself for being part of raising me-oriented kids, realize that every generation does the best they can with what they have. And it's in our nature to want better for our kids.

Sometimes in our effort to do better, we overdo. Remember that the responsibility doesn't rest solely on you as the parent. Don't get me wrong—we have a huge responsibility, but there are other factors to consider when raising kids. Society plays a big part in the development of any human. (Soapbox moment: For that matter, society even affects dogs. What a great time to be a dog, with little clothes and fancy food! The dogs of yesteryear are barking in jealousy from doggy heaven over today's lucky dogs.) I'm sure if my mom and dad could have picked a time to raise their kids, the late 1960s and early 1970s wouldn't have been their first choice. It was a rebellious time, as I've already noted. Not to mention, my poor mom spent hours at the sewing machine making beautiful dresses for my sisters and me, only to find them hanging in the closet while we wore the same pair of bell-bottom jeans day after day. Yes, society influences our choices.

Well, back to our topic of help. During an interview for *Playboy* magazine in 1980 (for the record, I didn't read it in *Playboy;* I found this on Wikipedia), John Lennon shared about the 1965 release of the song "Help!": "The whole Beatles thing was just beyond comprehension. I was subconsciously crying out for help."[2] Think about this. The world those four teenagers from England had known had been turned upside down. The tune released in 1965 to a frenzy that boggled the minds of parents everywhere. Girls screaming, fainting, and crying by the thousands. Who could handle attention like that?

My family has experienced it to a lesser degree with the success of *Duck Dynasty.* I remember our first meeting with producers, who told us our world would never be the same. We looked at one another and thought, *No, he doesn't understand. We're committed to keeping our lives the same.* And on many levels we have. We are all the same people with the same values, but as the saying goes, "You don't know what you don't know." We had no idea that the show would be really successful and that the family would be called to appear on talk shows, in magazine articles, and at red-carpet events. We couldn't have known that Sadie would appear on *Dancing with the Stars* and design a prom dress line and write books and give speeches and be in movies. We couldn't have known that homeschooling the kids for parts of the year would be in our future. We couldn't have known that our children would face hateful comments on social media. We couldn't have known that having a TV show makes it nearly impossible to go to the mall on a Saturday afternoon. We couldn't have known that if we did go to the mall with our celebrity family, we would see their faces on everything from Chia Pets to pajamas. Needless to say, our lives *did* change.

With any life change, whether it's a job, marriage, a new baby, retirement, or a TV show, we are challenged to grow, and many times growing means asking for help. And that is not bad news. In fact, it's good news. I hope John, Paul, George, and Ringo were able to get the help they needed as they faced millions of screaming teenagers and eager reporters. I hope they had grandparents in their lives to remind them that their talents were from God and to use them wisely. I hope they had moms and dads who spoke words of love over them, telling them that if it all ended tomorrow, they could come home.

I don't know whether that was the case for the Beatles, though I sincerely hope it was. But it should be for your children and grandchildren. Every day is a new adventure, especially for our grandchildren. I remember a shopping trip with John Luke when he was eight years old. We were going to the grocery store, and from the back seat of my car he said, "2-mama, I've learned three things in life." Of course, my ears perked up, because I couldn't imagine what three things an eight-year-old had learned. He went on to explain, "First, you have to work hard. Second, you have to play hard. And third, you have to expect the unexpected." Needless to say, I was amazed at such wisdom from my firstborn grandchild. (Then again, he was the first. Aren't all first grandchildren brilliant?) But there was more. He said, "Do you know which one is the hardest?" "No, buddy," I said. "Tell me." "Expecting the unexpected," he replied. Over the years, I have thought about his wise words again and again. I have analyzed them. I have written about them. I have added scriptures to them. But it was just his simple—or maybe more complex—way of saying what Forrest Gump said: "Life [is] like a box of chocolates. You never know what you're gonna get." No truer words have been spoken. Life has a way of handing us a chocolate-covered peanut when we are reaching for the one with caramel. And it's not that the peanut one is bad; it's just not what we were expecting.

In 2007, my son, Ryan, and his wife approached us with very sad news. They were ending their marriage. Saying I was devastated is an understatement. I was crushed! Divorce was not ever in our conversation as a family. Like all marriages, mine wasn't perfect. We had our ups and downs, and at times, it seemed as if the downs outweighed the ups. But divorce was never an option, and forty-seven years into it, I'm very thankful we didn't quit. When our son and his wife came to us with this news, I thought we could fix it. I thought they were reaching out for help. We gave our own advice, offered to pay for marriage counseling, and suggested they go away for a few days to regroup. But none of the offers were accepted, and within months, the marriage was over.

I remember a friend of mine calling me and saying, "How are you even getting up this morning?" Wow! That was a good question. In fact, there were many questions. How do we move forward as a family? What does this say about our work in ministry and with other families? How will our grandkids survive this? How will our son manage being a single dad? What can we do to help? We had never walked this walk. When my children were little, I often heard the expression "Kids don't come with instruction books." Boy, did we need instruction now! Potty training was one thing, but dealing with divorce . . . that's serious stuff! Our grandchildren were three, five, and seven at the time. *Formative years,* I kept thinking. How do we help them understand that both parents love them and that they will be okay but that divorce is not God's plan for marriage?

At one point my sweet five-year-old granddaughter looked up at me and said, "Will you help us?" Now, that's a heart-wrenching moment. Of course I would help them. There was never any doubt that my husband and I would do anything needed to help Ryan's family, which now looked very different than it had for nearly twelve years. But still the questions were many. In what ways do we help? Should they move in with us? Do I go over every day and cook and clean? How do I help without interfering with my son's family? After many tears, thousands of prayers, and ten years, I'm thankful to say many of those questions have been answered. The children are thriving and life is good.

As parents of adult children, we are constantly navigating the parent and adult-child world. Again, it's a world we've never known and a world without a rule book or instruction manual. It may not be divorce for your family; it might be whether you should knock when you go to your adult children's homes (in our family if someone knocks, we think he's lost his mind, but that's us) or whether it's okay to bring gifts to the kids when you visit. In any case, if we thought that once the kids moved out, we would be free from anything that resembles worry, we were sadly mistaken.

I learned a valuable lesson from my mom. (Okay, I've learned lots of valuable lessons from my mom. You'll get to read about many of them.) I learned it not because she spoke of it but because she lived it: Once you're a mom, you're always a mom. No matter how old your children are, you will always have a little tug at your heart when things are not going well for them. I read a quote one time that said a mother is only as happy as her unhappiest child is. And that's not too far from the truth. On the flip side, our joy is abundant as our children enter the adult world and successfully make their mark on society. Then our joy is *beyond* abundant when the grandkids arrive.

Another thing my mom taught me is that a big part of parenting is doing the immediate. Remember those days when your kids were growing up and you planned to leave work; run by the gym; pick up supper; and have a nice, relaxing dinner at home with the family? Then the phone rang, informing you that little Suzy threw up on the playground. All plans were canceled, and the immediate took over. That's being a parent. I have now decided the same rule applies to grandparenting. For most of my days as a grandparent, I do the immediate. For my grands who had a single dad for many years, I made sure his family had meals planned for each day. (I've already confessed I'm not the best cook, but I can make a kid happy with spaghetti, grilled cheese sandwiches, or sloppy joes). I helped Ryan with buying the kids clothes and getting school supplies ready each year. I've taken the kids to the doctor and to sporting events. I've done whatever needed to be done. His family never moved in with us, which I thought was the best decision. Staying in his own home allowed the kids to have Grandma's house as a special place for sleepovers and parties. Because he traveled for work, our house has been a second home for the kids, and we're overjoyed to be able to provide that for them. But this has been true for all our grandkids.

I often check with all three of my children to see what I can do to help. Of course, over the years, the needs have changed as the kids have gotten older. Now we don't juggle little bodies; we juggle big-kid activities. My daughter Ashley, who lives in another state, has added me to her family's calendar. *What does that even mean?* you ask. Good question. Google Calendar allows you to share your calendar with another person. When Ashley adds an event to her calendar, it automatically shows up on mine. This way I can keep up without constant texting or phone calls (however, we do this quite a bit too). If I look on my calendar and see that one of the children has a doctor's appointment, I can text to see how it went. If one has a ball game, I can send words of encouragement or go, if possible.

The immediate and the tangibles are the easy parts of helping when tragedies or emergencies happen, right? As women, we can jump right in and bake a cake, clean a house, or pick up kids from school. We can get jobs done. What is hard to get done is what goes on inside us—the internalizing of every possible what-if. Our mom brains want to think everything through so we can be absolutely positive we helped in every way possible.

Let's go back to that question of why kids don't come with instruction books. It took a few years, but I finally figured out that they do.

And that instruction book is the Bible. No, it doesn't give potty-training tips or a definitive answer for the controversial question of whether time-outs are an effective discipline tactic, but it does give us every answer for dealing with every relationship.

Grandparenting is another link in the relationship chain. It's not about baking cookies or teaching a grandkid to drive or attending every ball game. It's about developing a relationship that says, "You are loved." The goal of parenting and grandparenting is putting enough good stuff into the next generation that we feel they will be able to carry on what we started (remember that layered civilization analogy). We want to help this next generation to the degree they need to be helped but still leave them with plenty to figure out on their own. And finding that balance can be tricky.

I've met many well-meaning parents and grandparents who have a hard time with the word *no*. And I agree, it's hard to say no to those you love enough that you would give your life for them, but having their best interests at heart means you have to exercise your own form of self-control. I have seen grandparents bail out grandchildren who continually exhibit wrong behavior. This is not help; this is hindrance and enabling. As grandparents, we have to understand that saying no may be the best form of help we can give. Nope, not easy, but necessary on occasion.

Once, when Sadie was little, the family went to see the Disney movie *Spirit*. Sadie left her stuffed animal in the car and wanted Korie to go back and get it. Korie had her hands full with four little ones and determined that Sadie did not need her stuffed animal that day. As the grandmother, I could have easily "helped" the situation and gone to the car for the stuffed animal. If I had, Sadie would have been happy, but Korie wouldn't have been. You see, Korie is on a mission to raise good kids, not just happy kids. As the grandmother, I respected Korie's plan to do just that. I sat there and let that sweet little granddaughter pout and whine while her mom taught her a very valuable lesson: we don't always get what we want in life.

I tell you that story to let you know that help doesn't always come in the form of solving children's problems. It often comes in not solving them. Letting them work them out. Sadly, we are dealing with a generation of people who aren't very efficient at problem solving. Think about it. They don't face as many obstacles in simple daily living as generations in the past have. In many ways, they are not getting much practice at it.

When I was growing up, we had six kids and a grandmother sharing one bathroom. Getting ready in the morning was a problem we had to solve. Now, we didn't know it was a problem; it was just life for us. But because of our living conditions, we learned to problem solve. We learned to be efficient during our time in the bathroom; we learned to clean up after ourselves; we learned that others have a right to the same space; we learned that bathroom time wasn't a luxury moment for anyone. In that one life issue—sharing one bathroom—many lessons were learned without any lectures given. We figured it out. In today's America, many of those living-condition issues have been resolved, and we are happy about that. But we have to be mindful that things such as respect for others' space are taught in different ways. For those children who have their own room and perhaps even their own bathroom, we have to be *intentional* about teaching those principles that having only one bathroom taught.

Here's another example. Think about what it took to learn a new song that hit the Top 40 when we were growing up. We had to wait patiently all day for the new song to be played on the radio. When we heard it begin to play, we quickly grabbed a pencil and paper and wrote the words down as fast as our fingers would fly. If we were really creative and desperate, we had our friends lined up to do the same thing, with each friend getting a different line of the song. After a week or two, we might have all the words written down and could start singing along with the radio. Once again, life lessons were taught just by living. It boggles my mind how today we can hear new songs almost the minute they are released, as well as find the lyrics, the guitar chords, and the karaoke version, which in our day didn't even exist! Man, these kids have it easy!

Grandparents, we have a big job to do. We have to help this generation see the value of respecting one another's belongings, treating each person kindly, using their time wisely, being grateful for what they have, and on and on. These lessons won't be learned in the same way we learned them, but remember, it was our parents who told us how they walked to school in the snow uphill both ways and *we* were the ones who had it easy. In their minds, we were doomed to a life not much more successful than a slug's, but we rose above it. Our grands will too. And with us by their side, they will have plenty of help along the way.

———

Since becoming a grandmother, I have heard two views on helping with the grandkids. The first one goes like this: "My kids expect me to drop everything and take care of the baby. I raised my kids; I'm not interested in raising theirs." The second one is this: "I wish I could keep the baby 24-7. I have a hard time not thinking the baby is mine. I love her so much!"

Two very different views of our role as grandparents and both very valid. Helping in any area of life requires sacrifice. There will be times in your grandparenting journey that you will be asked to give up something to help out. Most of us agree that we would gladly do what is necessary in emergency situations. But in this stage of your life, you are likely just now getting to enjoy life as a couple. Don't feel guilty about saying no to your children when it's not an emergency.

★ ★ ★ ★
Rockstar
GRANDPARENTING

It's not about baking cookies or teaching a grandkid to drive or attending every ball game. It's about developing a relationship that says, "You are loved."

When my grands were little, we had a long list of babysitters from the church who helped us out. While I was often called on to keep the grandkids when my children were out of town on business, I rarely kept them when my kids went out for a date night. Keep in mind that when my grands were little, ten of them lived very close to me, which would have made babysitting on a Friday night crazy. That's when we called on our trusty babysitters. That way date night was free for my husband and me to enjoy as well. Many times we went out with our adult children, which kept our relationship fun and growing as well.

My sister-in-law, called J-mama by her grands, has kept her grandkids every Sunday afternoon for many years. That gives her son and daughter and their spouses a break and gives her valuable grandma time. They live down the street from us, and we love visiting with them on Sunday afternoons. J-mama works full time, making Sunday a great solution for them. J-mama's children also use sitters from the church and other family members when they need help, ensuring that J-mama isn't overwhelmed caring for five little ones.

Another important aspect of helping is understanding that many times what we perceive as helpful isn't. I know that's hard to hear. We go out of our way to do what we think is the helpful thing, but sometimes it's not. Maybe we should first consider why we're doing what we're doing. A young mom at our church was devastated after her mother came to help her after the birth of her second baby. The mother hadn't been able to come when her first child was born, so her visit was highly anticipated. The young mom envisioned her mother helping with the two-year-old and doing things like the laundry and cooking. But her mom declared she came to see the new baby and spent three days holding the baby and doing little else. The young mom was frustrated and exhausted when her mom's visit was over.

Grandmas, here is my opinion on that, and you can take it or leave it. Our first responsibility is to our children, the ones we raised. We need to look to see that what we are doing is helping them first and foremost. Our second responsibility is to help our grandchildren. In this situation, the adult child needed help. The grandchild was perfectly fine sleeping next to her mom or in her bed. The new mama needed her mom to help her in other ways besides holding the baby.

When my daughters and daughter-in-law had their babies, I would have loved to sit and rock all day, but that wouldn't have helped the young women I loved. I made sure houses were clean and clothes were washed and food was available. Notice, I said I made sure those things were done. I didn't always do the jobs myself, but often I did. I worked full time when all my grands were born. I wasn't always available, but I could check in to see what was needed and then make it happen.

Help can come in many forms. As moms, we pulled teeth, bandaged skinned knees, offered advice to complete an essay, made brownies, drove car pools, and much more. As tired as we were during those days, there is a tiny bit of sadness when they're over. There may even be a few years of bruised ego when you think no one needs you anymore. But grandchildren are notorious game changers, and your next chapter is about to be written by you and your grandchildren. Get ready. As Mighty Mouse used to say, "Here I come to save the day!"

Family is God's great design for teaching us how to live in a community. Ultimately, we aim to live in heaven with millions of other believers. God needs to get us ready for that glorious event. Until then, we need to keep on learning by helping others here on earth, and that starts with our families.

Do not withhold good from those who deserve it
when it's in your power to help them.

—Proverbs 3:27

A Hard Day's Night

I don't know where we got the idea that our later years would be more relaxed and stress-free than our younger years. I'm guessing it came from observation; however, very few young people pay any mind (an expression my grandma used to use) to old folks, except if the young folks are asked to do something for the old folks.

For instance, once I acquired a driver's license at the ripe old age of fifteen, it became part of my job to take my grandma, who lived with us and never learned to drive, to choir practice and to the grocery store for prune juice and pantyhose. In my teenage brain, I could think of a thousand things to do besides taking Grandma to run errands, but that was my duty as a grandchild. As a teen, my perceptions concerning old age were starting to take root. I probably turned the key in my 1968 Chrysler and thought how nice it would be for my grandkids to tote me around one day (like that's going to happen now!).

My other grandparents lived about an hour's drive from us. This was my Grandpa and Grandma Durham, whom I have already mentioned. Remember, she was a nurse and he was a carpenter who built the crate for the atomic bomb. I'm sure there are many other details of their lives that were interesting and important, but as a child, I didn't see them. When I was younger and living in Oklahoma, my mother took us to San Diego to see Grandma and Grandpa Durham, but those visits were all about Disneyland, Knott's Berry Farm, and the beach. When I was nine, our family, as well as my Durham grandparents, settled in Louisiana, and we were able to see them more often.

My formative years, when I was figuring out a grandparent's role, told me that grandmas make biscuits and other great things to eat and grandpas "tinker" around the house and allow grandkids to "straight up" eat the sugarcane growing in the backyard. While we ate sugarcane and played in the yard, our grandparents sat on the back porch and snapped peas or shucked corn while they talked about fishing and family members. In my mind, they were the perfect grandparents. They didn't have anything to do but watch us play and feed us.

Times have changed. Very few grandparents today snap peas and shuck corn, but I'm willing to bet that's not all my grandparents did either. Looking back, I'm sure the snapping and shucking were part of the life lessons all of us grandparents try to sneak in when we don't think a kid is noticing. I laugh now, thinking that my grandma probably told my grandpa to go round up some peas and corn so these city kids could learn about fresh vegetables. It's amusing that my song choice for this chapter, "A Hard Day's Night," was sung by millions of teenagers who had no idea what constituted a hard day's night. It would be many years before the screaming Beatles-maniac teens would face an all-nighter with a sick baby or a work deadline or a cross-country drive to see family. When I first learned the lyrics and belted them out in my living room, my mom and dad had to have been chuckling inside at their eleven-year-old singing "And I've been working like a dog."[1] I was eleven years old. Eleven! My dog didn't even work like a dog!

Oh well, such is life. Now here we are—baby boomers with children, grandchildren, and, for many, aging parents. We are fully aware of a hard day's night. More demands, not only on our time but also on our money, have hit close to home for many of us. Sitting on the porch and watching the world go by is rarely an option anymore. Most of us are part of the sandwich generation that requires more than two pieces of bread.

Sandwich generation is a term given to any generation that finds itself taking care of parents and children at the same time. My mother took care of three of my grandparents and still had her sixth child at home. Going back another generation, my great-grandparents lived with my grandparents. As far back as my family can remember, grandparents lived with their children. This is not new. What *is* new is what is now being called the "senior sandwich" generation. As the population has aged and stayed healthier, adults in their sixties and seventies are now caring for parents in their eighties and nineties. On the other end of the spectrum, many young adults are waiting longer to get married and start families and have returned home because of losing their jobs or advancing their education. This makes for busy days for many adults who are caring for aging parents as well as supporting their adult children whose lives are still unsettled.

And there's more to the story of us all working like dogs. The age for retirement with full benefits was set at sixty-five by the Social Security Act of 1935. At that time, the average life expectancy for men who reached sixty-five was around seventy-seven.[2] Today, according to the

National Center for Health Statistics, life expectancy for men who reach sixty-five is around eighty-four; for women it's around eighty-six.[3]

That means the money received from social security that was designed to last around twelve years now needs to last around nineteen years. You don't have to be a mathematician (and I'm not one) to see this isn't going to add up very well. It's no wonder that in our fifties and sixties, we're still working as if we're in our thirties or forties. Remember how much we loved the statement "Sixty is the new forty"? Well, as Dr. Phil says, "How's that working for you?" Not so well for many. With all the added benefits of living longer and staying healthier, having to work to keep the money train rolling isn't one of them.

What's a grandparent to do? How can we secure our future without working ourselves into an early grave? I'm going to level with you—the only thing worse than my cooking skills are my business skills, but I'm married to a pretty savvy businessman whose dad was a savvy businessman too. My father-in-law, Alton Howard (aka Papaw Howard), wrote a book called *Money Grows on Trees.* The saying is "Money doesn't grow on trees," but Papaw decided to put a new twist on the old saying. He talked about how to more effectively put money on your money tree. I'm going to save you a little time and energy and give you the key components of the book.

One of my favorite quotes from it is this: "It's okay to hitch your wagon to a star, but be sure you know how to unhitch it before it falls."[4] Many times our children and grandchildren are our "stars." We don't mind investing in them because we love them and want the best for their future. But even if love is the reason, it's not always the best decision to pour money into a child. Remember that word problem in math that you hated because you couldn't come up with an answer? Eventually the teacher told you that there wasn't enough information to answer it. Then you felt relief. *Yay!* you thought. *I'm not totally dumb! No one could answer it.* Look at your grandchildren as that math problem. It's not that you don't love them or want to invest in their future; you just don't have enough information to do so. Giving money to anyone when he or she is not prepared to handle it is never the right answer. I recently heard someone say that money never solves money problems. In other words, giving money to someone to solve her money problem rarely solves it. It just makes the inevitable last longer.

This is a principle many have learned through years of mission work. In the early years of mission work, when ordinary people, not preachers, were able to enter the mission field, everyone wanted to give food, clothes, and even money to solve the many problems third-world countries have. While giving things such as food and clothes solves an immediate problem, there is more to the story of poverty, and those of us who wanted to help had to figure that out. After much trial and error, we learned that no one is motivated to work hard and make it on his own when he is given stuff. Another quote from Papaw Howard is "You do not have to be caught up in the mistakes around you."[5] Praise the Lord. None of us has to stay trapped in whatever situation we find ourselves in. It might take time, but financial stability can be achieved by everyone. Here is some of Papaw's wisdom put into my own language.

Choose Wisely

In Galatians 6:7, the writer, Paul, said, "Don't be misled—you cannot mock the justice of God. You will always harvest what you plant." No matter what area of life you are working on, if you plant healthy seeds, you will reap a healthy crop. If you are working on your marriage but continue to make poor decisions regarding your behavior, your marriage will continue to suffer. I don't believe God sits in heaven and looks down on us and decides how and when to bless us. I believe God gives us the liberty to choose our behavior and then blessings and curses come from those decisions.

I love how this verse says we "cannot mock the justice of God." God is all truth, which is why we can trust Him. The things He created will always work as He created them. Think about this. He created gravity. It will always work. If you doubt that fact, what do you think would happen if you jumped off a two-story building? Your belief in the law of gravity doesn't change what gravity does. The same is true with fire and water. All of God's creations are dependable. This verse warns us not to test or mock what God has created. We will not come out on top. If we apply God's principles to any aspect of our lives, we will find success. By success, I mean that we will have a level of peace that comes from feeling as if the areas of our lives are under control. Success is not just about being financially stable but about having stability in every area—emotional, physical, and spiritual. Making poor financial decisions can lead to damage in all these areas.

How you spend your money will always be your choice. From the time your parents gave you your first fifty cents for an allowance, you got to be the steward of your money. Another one of my favorite grandkid stories comes from my grandson Asa. Asa is now eighteen years old, but at the time of this story, he was only five. All of us are familiar with little ones sneaking into their parents' bed at night. If you haven't experienced it in a while, you are probably smiling, remembering chubby toes, soft skin, and arms wrapped around your neck. You've forgotten about being kicked in the back, being squished to the side, and sleeping on four inches of the mattress. My son and his wife had spent too many nights cramped and stomped on and decided to do what any self-respecting parents would do—offer money. (Remember, we all have a choice.) My son sat his two children, ages five and three at the time, down one night for a little talk. He told them that if they stayed in their bed all night, he would pay them one dollar, but if they got into his bed that night, they would owe him twenty-five cents. Feeling rather proud and confident about his plan, he kissed them and put them to bed. The night held great promise. But around 2:00 a.m., the familiar pitter-patter of little feet was heard. Only this time it was followed by a clinking sound. Then a warm little body snuggled in for the night. The next morning Ryan discovered the source of the clinking sound. There on the nightstand were two dimes and a nickel. Asa had decided it was worth the money to share his parents' bed and paid his way.

I love that story. It has application to many areas of our lives, but for today's conversation, it reinforces the fact that we all have choices to make about where and when we spend our money. Asa was given the choice not only to lose money but also to make money, but the trade-off wasn't worth it. In his mind, no amount of money was worth sleeping in his own bed. While Asa was happy about his decision, his parents were not.

This is a money fact: you won't make everybody happy, no matter what you do with your money. First Timothy 6:10 tells us that "the love of money is the root of all kinds of evil." Sad, isn't it? That this one thing can cause such dissension in families that marriages break up, children don't speak, parents intentionally distance themselves from their kids, and grandparents feel guilty. Money is just a piece of paper or a shiny coin, but its ability to destroy is real.

On the other hand, money can bring great blessings. Papaw Howard (remember, he wrote *Money Grows on Trees*) was a man of great vision for growing successful companies. From his success, he created a Christian youth camp that after fifty years is still blessing lives today; he formed a radio ministry that continues to touch lives all over the world; he invested in our local church family, which is still a growing community of busy, godly people; he helped hundreds of missionaries, entrepreneurs, and those sick and in need. While money can be the root of all kinds of evil, it can also be the root of peace and joy and can open the door for ways to bless others.

You have to choose how to spend your money. I want to encourage you to start making good choices in regard to your grandkids. I'm thankful I have a husband who can think things through objectively. When our grandparenting journey began, we had one grandchild. Now we have fourteen. What can be done for one child can't always be done for fourteen. Choose wisely what you put into place when you have just one or two grandchildren. I have talked to many grandparents today who feel financially trapped by their grandkid obligations. What started out as a well-intended helping hand is now a source of financial strain and resentment for the grandparents.

We all love our grandchildren and want to help them in life, but wise choices about how we help them financially are critical to maintaining our position as the leaders of our families. When anyone—and

I mean anyone—is given too much financial help, an attitude of entitlement can seep in. I know having entitled kids is no one's goal, but it is the outcome when your role in life is to hand out money as if you're the banker in Monopoly.

If you haven't chosen wisely in this area, it's time for a new sheriff to come to town. Sit down with a person qualified to help you sort it all out, and then honestly tell your family what changes need to be made. Remember the Scripture verse that says "the truth will set you free" (John 8:32)? Once you start getting your finances in tip-top shape, you will experience freedom as you've never seen before.

Prepare Efficiently

Our family loves to ski. We are able to go only once a year, but it's one of our favorite family vacations. Here's the deal with skiing for us southerners: we have to be prepared! There is nothing more miserable than being freezing cold, which, apparently, is a given with snow. Skiing involves layers of clothes topped off with hats, gloves, and protective face gear. In fact, there is so much involved in getting prepared, one wonders whether it's worth it. But once the gear is in place and you're standing at the top of a snow-covered mountain, the morning's work of gathering up and pulling on fades away—replaced with a smile as you soak in the majestic view. Yep, the key to any pleasant mountaintop experience is in the preparation. Without the proper clothing and equipment, the joy of the scenery is overtaken by below-freezing temperatures, which results in whiny skiers. Not fun!

I turned on my TV one morning to these happy, positive words:

"Running out of money in your old age is brutal." Yikes! That's almost as bad as those warnings on your computer telling you your computer has a virus or sitting on a chairlift in a blizzard (I've experienced both, by the way). Not good news! Here's the reality: all those scenarios are scary, but they can be less traumatic with the proper preparation.

It's been said that there are no guarantees in life except death and taxes. Being unprepared for the two things that are inevitable seems like a crazy way to live, but many do that. (I've also seen a few folks up on the mountain in shorts and T-shirts, but that doesn't make them smart.) I decided to google the topic of retirement and found article after article stating that Americans are not properly prepared for their last ski trip on the mountain of life, to go back to my skiing analogy. Hats, gloves, and face masks might have been bought, but you might be headed up the mountain with no lift ticket. You see, on a ski trip, even if you have all your gear, if you didn't purchase a ticket to get up the mountain, you're not going anywhere. The guy on TV is right: facing our later years without money would be brutal!

This troubling trend that Americans are facing results from all the things we've already talked about: living longer, supporting kids and grandkids, credit card debt, and on and on. I have found the AARP site and its many articles on retirement full of great information that will guide you through the steps needed for a healthy retirement. Another good resource is a financial planner. Don't be afraid to contact someone in this position to help you prepare for the inevitable. Remember this principle: it's never too late to do the right thing.

We've been on many ski trips that have required a stop at the top of the mountain for extra hats and gloves. We didn't look at the potential for help and stubbornly ignore it because we chose poorly when we left the house that morning. No, we eagerly embraced the second chance to do it correctly. If you find yourself in need of help, don't be afraid to stop and get it.

Another great resource is financial wizard Dave Ramsey. I listen to him any chance I get. I love that his financial help workshops are called Financial Peace University. What a great title! Who doesn't want peace in every area of life? One definition of *peace* is "freedom from civil disturbance"[6]—quiet and tranquility. We loved that peace sign in the '70s, didn't we? We drew it on our notebooks while ignoring the teacher in class; we embroidered it on our jeans; we held up our two fingers in protest of something we knew little about. Time has now taught us what peace is. It's not a sign or a symbol. Rather, it is, as the definition says, a state of feeling free from anything that disturbs us. When you go to Dave Ramsey's website, you are given "everything you need to take control of your money."[7] You just need the right plan. The road to any peaceful situation is always knowing how to achieve it. Seek the help you need to gain financial peace. Don't face your future unprepared.

In Papaw's book, he said if you don't save and invest for yourself, no one will do it for you. He pointed out that we have been not a nation of savers but rather a nation of spenders, and he warned that this must change.[8] The longer you delay your savings program, the harder it will be to get on track. Some of you reading this book are in your forties—good for you. You have plenty of time to turn the train around, but don't delay. Those of you in your sixties will need a more drastic correction of your spending and saving patterns, but you can do it.

Make Plans for When You're Gone

Phil Robertson often speaks at our church. He tells his listeners that every one of us will end up six feet in the ground. When I've heard that message, many times I've wanted to stand up and say, "Please stop reminding me of this!" But it's just like our example of gravity; closing our ears to this truth doesn't make it false or make it go away. It is always true. We are all headed for the bottom of a grave.

Oftentimes I get melancholy and think about the complexities of life and death. I think about the many hours of work that go into a lifetime, only to have it all abruptly concluded by one breath—the last one taken, signaling that life on earth is over. I think about my sweet friend who died this past year after a long battle with throat cancer. Oh, how he loved life. He was a businessman, a worship leader, a father, a husband, a grandfather. My husband and I sat on the very bed he lived his last days in and went through all his finances with his grieving widow. What a blessing it was for my husband to tell her that her kind, devoted husband had taken good care of her. She didn't need to make a hurried decision about her future. She had time to decide the direction she wanted to go. Our friend had prepared for his own death in a way that secured the future of his partner in life.

When one spouse dies, many things change, and preparation is the key. But when both parents are gone, other issues crop up. When parents die and a will has not been drawn up, children are left without direction and money is wasted instead of benefiting them in areas such as obtaining an education, buying a home, or paying for health care.

Dying without a will means the state can decide what to do with your assets. For many, the decisions surrounding who will get their money or assets after their death is daunting enough that they choose not to face it at all. But remember, no decision is a decision. No decision means you have determined to let the state and lawyers decide what to do with what you worked hard to accumulate.

As the end of life came more in focus for my in-laws, I was grateful to have a front-row seat to a perfectly executed example of how to do this right. (After all, Papaw had written a book about it. Duh!) First, Papaw believed his children and grandchildren could and would make it on their own without his assistance. While Alton Howard was a man with plenty of money, no one expected him to hand out money, and he rarely did. There was an understanding that Papaw might help in a bind, but everyone knew it should be a last-resort request. Second, Papaw supported many good causes. He gave most of his money away. As the end of life was nearing for this great man, how did he handle it?

> ★ ★ ★ ★
> **Rockstar**
> **GRANDPARENTING**
>
> No job or position or amount of money will be worth it if everything at home isn't right.

In his wisdom, he decided his possessions would be more valuable to his grandchildren than money. This was not because his grandchildren were into more "stuff" but rather because these possessions represented who Papaw was and what his life was about. He labeled everything of personal value in his house, and the grandkids, through a name-drawing process, went over to the house and chose what they wanted to be theirs when Papaw was no longer on this earth. I remember the kids being sad thinking of that day becoming a reality. They loved Papaw and couldn't bear to think of him not being around. But Papaw handled it as if it were another day at work. He delighted in watching them choose. He laughed with them. Bargained with them. Reasoned with them. Shared the experience with them. It was a day full of happy memories, not sad ones. My son, Ryan, the piano player, now owns the piano that Papaw wrote many hymns on. Papaw's grandfather clock and cherished bookcases greet me at the door every time I go visit my daughter Korie, who is an avid reader and loves to display her books on Papaw's shelves. And our Ashley, who loves to invest in others, sets her dining room table at Christmas exactly as Mamaw Howard set hers, using her grandparents' finest china. All the other cousins have special things in their homes that remind them of their grandparents' love for them and of their life journey.

Many people who know our family and are aware of Papaw's success in business think he left his children and grandchildren money, but it isn't true. He left something better than money. He left a love for family, ministries that continue to grow and thrive, a sense of security because of our family's faith in God, songs and hymns that still speak to the hearts of believers, and a legacy that values people over possessions and love over everything else.

It was amazing to watch this process as somewhat of an outsider. After all, I was the in-law, not a blood relative. I was loved the same and cared for the same, but I wasn't Alton's daughter. I had married into the family. (Here's my warning on this: Know your position in the family. Don't let jealousy enter your family dynamics. It is a sure killer of any family love. If you need to, have a conversation in your head that reminds you that your parents and your in-laws can do what they want with what they have, and you can too. Don't be the one in the family who causes dissension over something as meaningless as money.)

Here's Papaw's final advice on creating a will. It's found in his book *Money Grows on Trees*.

Sit down and determine what you have by drawing up a list of your assets. Determine how and to whom you want to leave your estate. With this information, seek out a good lawyer who can appreciate your purposes and have him help you draw up your will. . . .

And never try to write a will yourself. The laws are complicated and change often. The small lawyer's fee will save your heirs many headaches and, most of all, will allow your wealth to continue to work after you are gone in the way that you would desire.[9]

Pretty good advice, I would say!

In a recent conversation with John Luke, he told me he wanted my husband and me to turn the giving away of our possessions into a scavenger hunt. He said to make it fun! This is just like him. He was, and is, always ready for an adventure. And he knows me well. He knows I love a good party and I love events that teach life lessons.

When he was growing up, we loved to plan parties and events together. One time he wanted to give a green Jell-O party. Everyone invited was required to bring a huge pan of green Jell-O. A small inflatable swimming pool was filled with green Jell-O, and the boys had a great time wrestling in the pool. I'm not sure what life lesson we taught the kids, but we grandparents learned that green Jell-O attracts ants that are very difficult to get rid of! We also learned how important it is to dream with our grandkids, even if it's a crazy dream that requires a little extra work on our part. I'm not sure about the scavenger hunt idea, but right now, it sounds pretty good. We'll have to see as the years roll on.

———

It's a reality that we're a busy, hardworking generation of people. But let's not forget about the other words in that Beatles song, the ones that tell us that when we're "home, everything seems to be right." No job or position or amount of money will be worth it if everything at home isn't right. Right? Hopefully by now (since you're a grandparent with some wisdom) you have learned this valuable lesson: if you are making a lot of money and your home life is falling apart, it is not worth it!

We've lived through the times when men worked and women were housewives and stayed home. When I was a young girl, my daddy went to work every day and my mom managed the household. Times have changed, and that is rarely the model today. As my good friend, writer, and speaker John Rosemond likes to say, "Times have always changed." And he's right. Times *have* always changed, and it's up to each generation to apply godly principles to the world it inherits.

———

**Whatever you do, work at it with all your heart,
as working for the Lord, not for human masters.**

—COLOSSIANS 3:23, NIV

Teach Your Children

Released in 1970 on the *Déjà Vu* album, this song was and is one of my favorites. Perhaps because even when I was a teen, my goal in life was to be a teacher and a mom, the lyrics resonated with my spirit. That, and I loved, loved, loved anything the band Crosby, Stills, Nash, and Young sang. And those harmonies! Masterful! Don't you agree? In fact, if you haven't heard this song in a while, check it out on YouTube. I just did. Love it! I wish I could remember what part of the lyrics I loved as a sixteen-year-old. The words that stuck out to me recently were "The past is just a good-bye."[1] In that one phrase, we understand why it's important to teach our children. Our past is nothing but something to wave good-bye to if we don't hand down what we've seen and heard to the younger generation to keep it going.

According to the website Songfacts, Graham Nash wrote the song thinking about his relationship with his father, who spent some time in prison. I don't know Graham Nash or his father, but I kind of, sort of, maybe know people. In my lifetime I have noticed that most of us either emulate what we were shown or go the opposite way. That can work for or against people.

We all know stories of young men and women who grew up in challenging situations but, as adults, chose a different path and were highly successful. And the opposite is true. We know adults who were taught well by their parents but tossed their value system out the window for a contrary lifestyle. Because this is true, there is never a reason to stop teaching our children well. The Bible makes this very clear in Deuteronomy 4:9–10:

> Watch out! Be careful never to forget what you yourself have seen. Do not let these memories escape from your mind as long as you live! *And be sure to pass them on to your children and grandchildren.* Never forget the day when you stood before the LORD your God at Mount Sinai, where he told me, "Summon the people before me, and I will personally instruct them. Then they will learn to fear me as long as they live, and they will *teach their children to fear me also."*

Some have said this is the most profound song ever written because of its message of generational hope for a better future. We've already talked about the importance of family and how family is our first look at community. If we don't show our children and grandchildren how to do life according to God's plan, who will? This means that, as adults, we are in teaching mode nearly all the time.

I realize this can be exhausting. I understand that sometimes we just do not want to be responsible anymore. I remember those days as a mom when I didn't want my children to say my name ever again! I was overwhelmed with "Mom," "Mom," "Mom" being said by three needy children. Then they stopped calling my name so much. Then they grew up. Before I knew it, they were making decisions on their own and applying the things I taught them. And they didn't need me so much.

Soon the grandkids came along. I once again put on my teaching hat and waited to be needed to answer a question or teach a lesson or show how to make or mend something. In my later years, I understand more clearly the wisdom that comes from God and Crosby, Stills, Nash, and Young. Teaching our children to live by the code we have lived by is the number one goal we should have in life—before making a lot of money, sticking to any diet, building a new house, running in a marathon, or anything else.

Will all of them get it? Maybe not. It's not our responsibility for them to get it, but it is our responsibility to give it.

What's the Lesson Plan?

What are some of the things we need to teach our children? How do we teach without being preachy? I'll tell you just a few things we have thought important to teach our children and grandchildren. Your list might be different, but that's okay. Your family operates as your family, not mine. Here we go.

How to Be Hospitable

My parents and my husband's parents were leaders in the field of hospitality. If houses could have revolving doors on them, these two houses should have had them. My children grew up watching their grandparents feed and house people from all backgrounds. My husband's father loved to sing. Old-fashioned "singings" were frequently held at their house, as well as Sunday dinners featuring Mamaw's famous roast and mashed potatoes. My parents were equally hospitable. Large and small gatherings were frequently held at their house. To this day, my mom hosts a house church every Sunday evening, even though her life partner, my daddy, has been gone for many years now.

Grandparents, I love that we get to be more involved with our grandkids than grandparents of the past. It's an absolute joy with a capital *J*! But let's remember that our lives continuously teach these littles how to do life. The practice of hospitality is a biblical principle that teaches us to put others first, to care for others, to serve others. When our grandchildren see us respecting this biblical principle, they see Jesus in action.

Naturally, my husband and I live in different times and are different people from our parents. My husband doesn't have the gift of singing his dad had, and I don't make an awesome roast and mashed potato dinner like his mother—which gives our hospitality a different look. We have been blessed with a house large enough to host families who are in need for a time. Over the years, we have had more than eighty people live with us for a short time (six months to over a year) while they waited for their house to be built or needed to go to school in our area or had a job that wasn't going to be permanent. We are blessed to be able to help in this way and consider our house to be God's house. Our home is often called the Howard Hotel. We've also hosted hundreds of parties, weddings, and showers, and our house is the permanent location for Sunday night "teen church" for our local congregation.

Hospitality is a mind-set; it's not a one-size-fits-all T-shirt. It's being willing to let others into your life. *Merriam-Webster* defines it as "generous and friendly treatment of visitors and guests." Notice it doesn't say having someone over every Sunday or letting complete strangers stay at your house. No, the dictionary is like the Bible on this one—it's up to you to decide how hospitality is carried out.

In ancient days, being hospitable meant lodging a weary traveler or tending to a widow or clothing the poor. Sharing a meal in biblical days meant creating a special bond with that person. We're deliberately told Jesus ate with tax collectors and sinners (see Mark 2:15). And think about Jesus choosing to feed the five thousand (see Mark 6:30-44). Jesus had the opportunity to show those people what love looks like by hosting a meal of fish and bread.

I can't tell you how many meals of fish and bread Phil and Kay Robertson (my Robertson grands' grandparents) have shared with the lost, the lonely, and those looking for answers to life's problems in our area. Their door has always been open to share the good news of Jesus through a meal of fish and hush puppies. I'm grateful that my grandchildren have seen this generous spirit through all their grandparents. Hosting a meal or lodging a friend in need shows others what love looks like, and our grandchildren take note of this. Oh, they might not tell you they notice, but they do.

How to Use Words for Good

We have all heard it said that words are a powerful tool. When I was a child, my dad spoke in idioms. Did yours? For example, if I told my dad I wished I could go somewhere or get something, he would likely reply, "If wishes were horses, then beggars would ride."

"What?" I might ask, puzzled at this response. Then he would do the strangest thing. He would just repeat it. No explanation. *Nothing!* I was left to figure it out on my own (more problem-solving opportunities). And guess what? Maybe I figured it out on the spot or maybe, years later, I understood.

One of the idioms my grandmother always said was "Pretty is as pretty does." Remember that one? Without lecturing, this was a great way to tell a child that how she acts is way more important than how she looks.

Here's one more. Johnny's dad and my dad were both notorious for the "Money doesn't grow on trees" saying. In five simple words it tells children, "You can't get anything you want because I don't have an endless supply of money for you." No explanation needed. You, child, figure it out.

I've often wondered, *How is it possible our generation didn't see the value of these short, simple responses?* (Oh yeah, I forgot about our rebellious nature.) Yes, it was someone from our generation or someone speaking into our generation who decided those idioms didn't work at all. Instead, we brilliantly thought we should give children an explanation for any decision, rule, or command we wished them to carry out. *What were we thinking?* Wouldn't you like to know who thought of that crazy parenting technique? Here we stand, right in the middle of the "explanation" era of parenting. Idioms, short sayings, even that famous look your parents used on you that achieved good results have all gone by the wayside.

Well, I'm here to tell you that words matter. Words have the power to make or break a person.

When I was in college, I took an art introduction class required for all freshmen. The first day, the teacher, who was known for her down-to-earth style of communicating, said something that totally changed my life. I seriously can't tell you one other thing I learned in her class, and I think it's better than knowing who painted the *Mona Lisa* (okay, I do know that one). She was lecturing us about not being tardy to her class and said, "If you are tardy, just walk in the room and take your seat." She continued, "I know what you're thinking. You're thinking you don't want to walk in late because you don't want everyone to look at you. Well, get over it. Who are you to think everyone is going to look at you in the first place?"

Whoa! I thought. *That's me.* I was an extremely shy child, and by college I still had not figured out how to live as a shy person and accomplish big, bold things. I was the one who would not walk in late for fear of everyone looking at me. I was the one who wouldn't raise my hand even if I knew the answer. I was the one who didn't speak up if I was given a grade I knew I didn't deserve. But I didn't think of myself as arrogant or self-absorbed until this teacher told me I was.

From that day forward, I've checked my shyness at the door and proudly walked into the room early or late. (Okay, maybe I carry my shyness with me, but I go in anyway, telling myself no one cares to look at me. Everyone has his or her own issues to think about.)

The power of words. Each of you reading this book has a similar story. Maybe it was a preacher, a Sunday school teacher, a friend, or a grandparent whose words had an impact on your life, but I know it happened. As grandparents, we are in a position to completely change the life of a child with a few carefully chosen words—and millions of other ones thrown in just for fun. The ability to use words is what makes us human. I love that.

Let's go back to the pet analogy. Did I mention this craziness yet?

Oh yes, I talked about dogs not being able to name us. Guess what else they can't do. They can't talk to us. They can wag their tails and tilt their heads as if to question us, and they can obey an order given by us, but they cannot respond to us with words. God gave words to us. "Humans only," God surely declared as He scanned the creatures He had made. He gave us words and the power to communicate with, encourage, and inspire one another.

Recently my granddaughter Sadie was in town. She asked my mom and me to go to lunch with her. We spent an hour listening to her dating life and telling her about our dating experiences. Who doesn't like a good love story? Sadie did. Your grandchildren will too. Sadie sat fascinated while she listened to her great-grandmother tell how she dated her future husband's best friend for a year before she could ditch him and marry the man of her dreams. From a simple love story, Sadie learned about patience, devotion, sensitivity, hope, and good manners. We all laughed thinking of Mamaw Jo scheming of a way to get her current boyfriend out of the picture and letting our sweet Papaw Shack take his place. Mamaw's story encouraged Sadie to keep doing what she's doing, and it let her know that God will honor her deepest desires and dreams.

Our life examples are like a group of kids lined up to jump off the high diving board. Each kid's actions encourage the next kid to do the same. Watching or hearing about the success of others empowers us to accomplish that task as well. Your stories tell your grands that if you can do it, so can they.

Whether it's in short idioms with powerful messages or long stories of faith, hope, and love, words matter and change lives. Words inspire, motivate, correct, heal, empower, and comfort.

Grandparents, we have the greatest job ever, don't we? Not only do we get to have lots of hugs and snuggles, but we also get to make a difference in the lives of some pretty special people. We get to tell the stories and connect the dots for the future generation. Don't waste this time. Don't store your stories away in photo boxes and never take them out. Use mealtimes for story time. Use car rides for encouragement time. Write, text, or share over Snapchat words of love and encouragement, or just send a joke. Your grands need a reason to roll their eyes that day. If you want to be a part of your grandchildren's lives, *show* them how to communicate.

One way we do this in our family is with organized table talk at dinnertime. It's not as if we don't have enough to talk about, but the kids love it when we ask a question that everyone has to answer. Questions such as "What would be your perfect day?" or "What is your favorite rock song, and why?" or "If you could go anywhere, where would it be?"

These questions encourage conversation and let everyone in the family get to know one another better. You can easily make up questions yourself and put them in a jar. The kids love to take turns being the reader of the question.

Another thing we do is called "ups and downs." We go around the table and let each person share an "up" and a "down" time that day or that week. Again, it's a great way to encourage conversation and lets each child open up about his world.

Whatever you can do to encourage real, face-to-face talking, do it!

How to Love Unconditionally

When my first grandchild was born, I was just like all of you—I was crazy in love with that baby! I will never forget seeing him for the first time. He wiggled his perfect little mouth, and his cheek formed the perfect little dimple. We all squealed in delight. The hallway of our local hospital was crammed with family all trying to get a glimpse of the most perfect baby ever born. Those dimples, those hazel eyes, those sweet toes—every aspect of him was absolutely perfect. At forty-two, I felt way too young to be a grandmother and, I'm sad to admit, even hesitated to tell others I was about to be one, but as soon as John Luke Robertson made his appearance, all that changed. I was a grandmother! I completely forgot how old the word *grandmother* sounded. On October 11, 1995, it said nothing but *love*!

It's true, when a grandbaby is born, busy schedules stop, cameras flash, and tears flow. No red-carpet event surpasses the arrival of a grandchild. Loving our newborn grandchildren is the easy part of maintaining and growing love in a family. Grandbabies make any verse on love seem easy. Who doesn't love babies who coo, smile, snuggle, and even seem to prefer you over their own mom? It's the best! But maintaining that level of excitement and joy can be tricky in today's busy world.

Mostly, love takes time. It's an investment in another person. No matter how many shortcuts we have acquired in the twenty-first century, we still complain that we don't have enough time. I remember when computers came on the scene. My youngest brother, Jeremy, had a knack for computers and took classes until he became the expert at the private school where we taught. I clearly remember him telling us that computers weren't designed to give us more time; they were designed to help us use our time more effectively. That must be true of all inventions. I'm sure the women who were around when washing machines came out thought they would have more free time, and I'm sure they were disappointed to discover that other responsibilities quickly took that time.

My daddy always told me, "You've got the same twenty-four hours in a day that the president has. Do your best to make them count." *True,* I would think as I grudgingly went back to my homework or chore for the day.

As grandparents, we might have more free time than we once had, but many of us still lead busy lives. Being busy isn't an excuse for not showing love. Love is many things. While it is a feeling supported by actions, it's also a fact that can be depended on. I might not have always used the right words or acted as I should have, but I prayed that my children always knew I loved them. That fact should have never been doubted. This is a valuable lesson that can carry over to our walk with God. How do we know God loves us? Do we always feel His love? Probably not, but those of us who believe the Bible trust that its words are true, and the Bible tells us that God loves us—even when we feel unlovable or unloved, even when our hearts are heavy with grief or despair. In those times, we lean on what we know is true. The fact is, you love your grandchildren, and that fact alone will give them peace and hope in times of trouble. It will also teach them and reinforce for them the attributes of God.

Loving your grandchildren unconditionally might seem like an easy task, especially as you rock that newborn baby, but there will be challenging and difficult days ahead. There will be days when grace and patience must be abundant. On those days, remember to look at that child with the same eyes God looks at you.

How to Pray

The greatest gift you can give your grandchildren is to pray for them and to show them how to pray. When I was growing up, my grandmothers never verbalized that they were praying for me. It wasn't that they didn't pray; it just wasn't spoken about. In the 1950s and '60s, it was just understood that your parents and grandparents prayed for you. My parents and my husband's parents were more vocal about it to my children. My husband's dad was a businessman, preacher, songwriter, and prolific writer of devotional messages that he emailed to many who loved his words of wisdom. In both our families,

If we don't show our children and grand-children how to do life according to God's plan, who will?

prayer was said at all meals, whether at home or in a restaurant. All our children carry on this important tradition in their families. Prayer has always been a big part of our faith walk.

When my granddaughter Macy had her tonsils removed, she had a tough recovery. She was eighteen at the time, so we knew this experience might be rough, but we had no idea how rough. After the initial surgery, we got her settled in at home for a quiet day of taking care of her needs. All went well until midnight (why is it always midnight?) when she began to bleed. The rest of the night was spent in an ER room, then in an ambulance to another hospital, and next in surgery to stop the bleeding. Just before her surgery, a very frightened Macy asked me to pray for her. I felt so honored that she chose me to cover her in prayer.

There will be plenty of emergency prayers as your grandchildren go through childhood and the teen years, but what can you do on a daily basis? I don't like the "Please be with all my grandkids" prayer that I often utter just before I fall asleep, but trust me—it does happen. I try hard to be more deliberate and specific, but with fourteen to think about, I admit I'm reduced to the minimum on occasion.

Since not all my grandchildren live close to me, it's impossible to attend every sporting event, school program, or doctor's visit, but I can pray. Many people have asked me how I keep up with everyone. I don't always, but I try. Here are my "hacks" (new word for "tips"—your grandkids probably say this) for knowing what my grandkids are doing and what I should be praying for:

1. *Get on social media.* Seriously, boomers, it's not that hard. Many of you are on it and are functioning like twentysomethings. Good for you! But some of you are resisting it, telling yourself it's for the kids. You are right—it's for the kids, and that's why you have to be there too. That's where your kids and grandkids are, so you need to join the party! It's perfectly okay to stalk your family members and see what everyone is up to. But don't just stalk them; use a stalk/pray technique. One of the blessings of social media is being able to see where your grandkids are and what they are doing in real time. No more waiting for a letter to arrive four days after an event happened. I can instantly pray when I see a teen grandchild on the lake with friends or headed to a party. It makes me feel better to cover her in prayer when I see her with a group of teens. Even better, I might text her that I'm praying she'll have a safe and fun time. Another thing we do as a family is have a group Snapchat. I know all the controversy over Snapchat, and my younger grands certainly don't have it, but since my older ones are on there, now I am too. Our family Snapchat brings lots of laughs to our day and helps us all stay connected.

2. *Have a shared calendar.* I already mentioned this, but as a reminder, I use this for my grands who live in another state. I am connected to their parents' calendars through Google Calendar. It's a great way to know what everyone is doing on any given day. If Macy has a doctor's appointment, I can pray about it right then and call or text afterward to check on her. If Ally has tennis practice, I can check in that night to discuss what she learned. It's awesome! Check it out.

3. *Call them.* Okay, go old school: pick up your cell phone and call your kids or grandkids. It still works. You get to talk to a live person. I absolutely love it when my phone rings and one of the grands is calling. They may not feel the same way about me calling them, but I do it anyway. If they are busy, they always text and we set up another time to talk. (I invariably call John Luke as he is sitting down for class at college. It's now become a joke, because it's happened so often.) I try to keep it quick; I ask them about their day, tell them I'll be praying for whatever they have coming up, and tell them I love them. Usually I blow a kiss if we're FaceTiming, sending an extra dose of love.

Start and end each day in prayer. Without them ever knowing, start and end the day praying for your family; then try to let it go. I had a recent conversation with a grandmother whose grandchild is making terrible choices. The situation is beyond what she is capable of helping with, except through prayer. There are many grandparents in this situation, and my heart goes out to them.

For those times when you feel as if you've said it all and don't know how to pray for a particular child, try praying Scripture over him. For example, I love Isaiah 40:31, so I might pray this way: *Lord, I pray my grandchildren learn to trust in You and soar higher than the eagles and learn to run and not grow weary and walk and not grow faint. Stand beside my grandchildren. Give them strength and courage and hope. In Jesus's name, amen.*

The Crosby, Stills, Nash, and Young song flips at the end and tells children to teach their parents well. We all know that our children do teach us. It's in having children that we become who God needs us to be. I've always said being a parent requires the patience of Job and the wisdom of Solomon and the grace of God. As grandparents, we have acquired a little more patience, wisdom, and grace. It's with honor that we get to apply these to our grandchildren and continue the journey of teaching the next generation well.

———

Train up a child in the way he should go [teaching
    him to seek God's wisdom and will for his
    abilities and talents],
Even when he is old he will not depart from it.

—PROVERBS 22:6, AMP

The Sound of Silence

*I*n many movies, life for the leading lady begins with a challenge. Such was the beginning for Princess Tiana in a Disney movie I took my two youngest granddaughters to when they were seven years old. The movie was *The Princess and the Frog*. Tiana had spent her life struggling to work her way up in the world and was given the opportunity to kiss a slimy frog with the hope of him becoming her handsome prince. But the kiss brought her only more trouble—one look at her hand and she shrieked as she discovered she had joined him in the frog kingdom. There would be no handsome prince. She was now a frog! As the prince and the leading lady hopped their way through the perils that plague tiny green creatures, my granddaughter Aslyn leaned over and whispered, "I know they will become people again." To which I replied, "How do you know?" Without a moment's hesitation she responded, "Because every princess story has a happy ending."

My heart nearly stopped at those incredibly misguided but hopeful words. I could hardly concentrate on the rest of the story as I thought of Princess Diana. I wonder whether she began her fairy tale with Prince Charles *knowing* she would have a happy ending. After all, all princess stories have a happy ending, don't they? As rumors of infidelity followed Diana's prince, did she still think a happy ending was in her future? As the divorce became final, did she still see a happy ending? When the ill-fated car pulled onto the busy street in Paris, did a happy ending play out in her mind? Oh, if only happy endings were the fate of all princesses.

Fairy tales and real life rarely match up. Am I right? In 2009 we spent three months in England, roaming the countryside, visiting castles and manors and palaces. The beauty of each structure was breathtaking, certainly as majestic as any Disney movie could reproduce. But the stories told of the kings and queens who reigned over their castles and kingdoms were not those depicted in Disney movies. Happy endings were rarely their fate. In fact, it would have been in one's best interests to turn down an offer to become any part of royalty back in the days of castles and kings and queens.

As an aging baby boomer, I have lived long enough to know hard times, up close and personal. I have buried those whom I love and miss every day. I have cried through broken marriages. I have sat by the bedsides of those too sick to hold their heads up. Death, divorce, and disease are not happy endings. You see, happy and sad endings are a part of life for everyone—those with crowns and those without.

Simon & Garfunkel released "The Sound of Silence" in 1964. It was just one of many songs by the greats of that era whose lyrics reflect times more tragic than any of us boomers had experienced. We didn't grow up with kingdoms being overthrown or men being chased by lions in large arenas. We weren't even children who experienced breadlines with parents who couldn't find work. We were children of the

1950s and '60s. It was a happy time in America. After all, the TV show depicting our era was named *Happy Days*. Our moms wore pearls to vacuum, and our dads looked dapper in their suits and ties as they headed out the door to work. Okay, maybe your mom didn't wear pearls (mine didn't either), but our moms proudly cooked, cleaned, sewed, disciplined their children, and loved their husbands. A few moms worked outside the home, but most were known as housewives because they worked at keeping the home running smoothly. My dad did wear a suit to work and, like most dads of that time, worked hard to pay the bills and keep the yard looking good. He threw a baseball to his sons and tucked his daughters in bed at night. Men like him were proud to be dads and the leaders of the family.

But something about all that didn't seem to be enough. Perhaps it was nothing more than the cycle of life that caused our generation to live with happy days but sing about days more melancholy. Songs that dug deep into our souls were at the top of our playlists (or in our record collections). They challenged who we were and where we were going and what we hoped to accomplish. They caused us to sit around bonfires and sing softly while a guitar-playing friend strummed the latest hits. Some of the songs whispered to us that all was not right with the world and we should do something about it. This led to disruption and rebellion, causing hours of grief to parents who were confused and left wondering what they'd done wrong. But in the end, maybe it was just cyclical. It's how things go around in life. What one generation values, the next doesn't. Maybe it was just time for a generation to question, and we did. Everything.

Songs of both silence and rebellion were a part of our generation.

We heard people say, "Don't trust anyone over thirty." No wonder our parents were nervous. It's funny to us now, isn't it? Thirty-year-old people today have a hard time admitting they're adults, yet we were told not to trust the adults over thirty!

In my research to find out what is behind the haunting lyrics of "The Sound of Silence," I learned that the facts are vague. Art Garfunkel once summed up the song's meaning as "the inability of people to communicate with each other, not particularly internationally but especially emotionally, so what you see around you are people unable to love each other."[1] It's very 1960s, isn't it? Peace and love were the battle cries of this generation. But were we really that disconnected? After all, we played outside daily with friends from the entire neighborhood. We ate nearly every meal around the kitchen table with every family member present. We attended church every Sunday and usually had another family over to share lunch with us. We talked on the phone (the one that hung on the kitchen wall) for hours to our friends. Seems as if we had a handle on communication.

Perhaps the lyrics are more appropriate in today's culture. Remember the lines that said people were "hearing without listening" and "writing songs that voices never share"?[2] It's a little like the line in *Cool Hand Luke*. Remember that movie? (Of course you do—you're a grandparent.) "What we've got here is failure to communicate." Failure to communicate is a tragic state to be in, and let's face it: we're on the brink of that happening in society today. It doesn't take long to look around a group of people, young and old, and notice no one is communicating. No one is sharing her life with anyone else. Our smartphones get all our attention.

Grandparents, we have to help change this. We are the only genera-tion left on earth that remembers the days of riding in a car without seat belts. Our only defense was Mom or Dad yelling, "Hang on!" We're the only generation that remembers when an attendant would come to our car window and we'd say to him, "Fill it up, please." (And it cost only two dollars for a whole tank of gas!) We're the only ones left with mem-ories of every family in the country eating around their dinner table at approximately the same time. Remember that? All the kids on the street went into their houses for dinner at the same time.

With fourteen teenage and early twenties grandchildren, I witness this lack of communication all the time. A crowd of young people on their phones, not talking to one another. Or with earbuds in their ears, not talking to one another. Or playing a video game, not talking to one another. Was this song before its time? Or has communication with others always been a challenge?

The Bible does warn us about controlling our tongues, and in Ecclesiastes we're told there's "a time to be silent and a time to speak" (3:7, NIV). A current joke goes like this: "I'm having a few folks over Saturday to look at their phones. Want to come?" This joke is a sad—but true—commentary on today's life.

As grandparents, the leaders of the pack, what is our role in this new age of communicating, or lack thereof? We've talked about this a little in an earlier chapter, but I have a few more thoughts to lay out. Here we go.

I confess I'm on my phone way too much. Our phones are our calendars, our computers, our calculators, our dictionaries, our encyclo-pedias, our entertainment, and our news and information source. We're all guilty. Learning to live with new inventions, figuring out how to regulate new technology, and educating ourselves on when to exercise our gift of silence or speaking will always haunt parents and grandparents who care about the state of the world they live in. Some don't care. I do.

I have another confession: I struggle with knowing when to be quiet and when to speak up. I am a paradoxical person. I am both opinionated and shy. How does that work, you ask? Well, not easily. It means I think of a lot of things to say, but I'm too shy to say them. Truly, I don't think I'm overly opinionated. Maybe I'm overly helpful. *Maybe?*

I do know I've been a problem solver from way back. My first real glimpse of it was when I was fifteen years old. My older sister and I were minding our own business, lying out in the sun in our backyard. (I know. We probably were lathered in baby oil. More bad things from the '60s.) We could hear the soft music of the ice cream truck going by. It was a perfect day. Then, all of a sudden, we heard squealing tires and children yelling our sister's name. You guessed it. Our five-year-old sister had been hit by the ice cream truck. It was terrible. Almost as suddenly as the wreck occurred, I went into fix-it mode. I ran inside and called the ambulance, got our mother, and ran back out to check on Jessi. She was badly injured with a broken leg, which she did recover from after a lengthy hospital stay and a body cast. We were all in shock that day, but no one more than me.

I was shocked at myself. Where did my immediate response come from? I've already mentioned I'm the shy one. My older sister was the one who usually took control—bossy, we thought as kids. She was the strong leader of us six kids. When Mom and Dad were gone, she was in charge. But that day she couldn't move. I knew it was up to me to get help, so I did. Perhaps that was the pivotal point to my feeling the need to help everyone. As I was typing this, my daughter Ashley sent me a picture of her hand with a deep cut on it. She had dropped the blade to the blender on it. Now, keep in mind she lives in Huntsville, Alabama, yet she was asking me what to do and I gladly told her.

You tell me you can't figure out how to get one child to tennis, one to gymnastics, and one to a birthday party all at the same time, and I'll tell you how to make it happen. You tell me your child won't go to sleep at night, and I'll give you a list of three things to try. You tell me your flight leaves at 3:45 and arrives at 5:10, and I'll tell you whether to take Uber or a taxi to the hotel. Maybe that's why I love math. Math is problem solving. I'm sure I'm spinning this to appear as if this is a good trait, but no doubt my kids have secretly rolled their eyes when I go into lecture number 936 about how to raise kids or clean a toilet.

Duck Dynasty

For the first two and a half years of filming *Duck Dynasty,* I was the on-set tutor for the kids. When a show is filming with minors, the law says that a certified teacher must be on the set at all times the children are there. When we were first told this, it took about ten seconds to decide the tutor would be me. Problem solved. The kids were still young, and we were inexperienced at filming a reality show. Naturally, we thought it would be good to have someone who knew the kids on set with them. Plus, I would be there to speak up if the kids were asked to do anything they were uncomfortable doing. (Fortunately, that didn't happen. But I was there just in case.) Plus—*plus*—I wanted to do it! And as luck (or God, for sure) would have it, I have a degree in education. In fact, my teaching years included an in-school tutoring program for kids of all ages, which meant I had tutored nearly every subject up to eleventh grade. *Thank You, God, for that chapter of my life.* At the beginning of filming, the Duck Commander kids ranged from two to sixteen, which meant I was qualified for the job.

The first day I was asked to be at filming, I was very excited. The scene called for the kids to help Papaw Phil clear some debris from a field to get it ready for a family football game. I remember getting the information about what time I should arrive and calling Korie to discuss this new adventure. She had already filmed a few scenes, so I knew she would tell me how fun it was and what to expect. "Mom, listen to me," she said in her I'm-trying-to-be-serious voice. "Do not try to tell them how to do *anything*. You will get annoyed that it's not running as smoothly as you want it to run, but don't say anything. Keep quiet."

Wow! There it is. The warning the Bible talks about—apparently this was going to be a time to be silent. I'm sure this wasn't the first time I needed to be silent, but it was the first time one of my children asked me to keep quiet in such a direct way. In our family we never used the words "Shut up." "Be quiet" were the strongest words one could use without getting in trouble. I think Korie was pretty close to using the *s* word ("Shut up") that day.

My daughter, who knows me all too well, knows that I hate it when things don't run smoothly and that I can usually think of a thousand things that could be done differently when something isn't working efficiently. I could, no doubt, "fix it." In my defense, I am the second born of six children, giving me some right to leadership and organizational skills, *and* I have been the director of a summer camp for more than thirty years, which requires wearing many hats, *and* I was a schoolteacher. Schoolteachers have mad organizational skills! Still, none of that mattered. The production team didn't care that I was an experienced grandma with many talents, some of which could have seriously helped them. No, they didn't care that with a whistle and a bullhorn I can get over two hundred middle schoolers through a lunch line in twenty minutes—tops. They didn't even care that I took my organizational skills to the swimming pool as part of a synchronized swimming team and finished my senior year swimming to the 5th Dimension song "The Age of Aquarius." They didn't even ask whether I had ever taken my grandchildren—all of them under ten at the time—to a movie and successfully bought them snacks, visited the bathroom, and got them seated before the previews started. If they only knew!

But alas, they saw me only as the old grandma hovering over her grandkids and protecting them from the perils of Hollywood. That is what my job was for the day. Following instructions, I arrived at the place in the woods and found my spot to sit and watch—not to offer advice, just to sit and watch—my grandkids film, for the first time, on reality TV.

It was hard. Korie was right. There were a thousand things they could have done differently, but it wasn't my place to tell. Finding our place in our new role as grandparents is a constant battle. From the time that new baby comes home and you ache to hold him all day every day, when you long to step in with good old-fashioned words of wisdom, you will be challenged to keep quiet. Many nights, as my grands are teens now, my husband asks me whether I should speak to one of them about a post he saw on Instagram or something he heard one say to a friend. Not bad things, but things he thinks they might be struggling with or could use a little guidance on. I always tell him we should wait and see what happens. Most of the time things work themselves out.

Here's the reality. Even if you are a parenting expert with books to your credit, you should keep quiet until you are specifically asked and then, only then, proceed with caution. What your children need more than advice and correction are love, affirmation, and cheerleading. They need a voice that will confirm to them that they are doing okay. They don't need your two cents on everything from rocking a baby to giving a teen an allowance. They need you to tell them they are raising great kids and you are proud of them. They need you to be willing to give advice but not be overly eager to share it if they aren't ready to listen. It's better to let them think you don't know anything than be aggravated that you think you know everything.

If you're a person who likes lists, I've put together a list that might help you navigate the sound of silence required by grandparents.

1. When in Doubt, Don't Speak Out

If you have any doubt that what you're about to say might come across as rude, arrogant, invasive, or self-serving, don't say it. For instance, never say, "When I was breastfeeding, I never had any trouble" or "When you were young, I made sure you had a nap every day." And definitely never say anything that shows disrespect for actions the parents are taking. Even if you don't agree with them, tell yourself that all adults alive today were raised differently than you raised your children and they all made it to adulthood.

Be careful not to use the word *why* to begin a conversation in which you intend to be helpful. Using this word makes the other person feel as if she has to defend her position. For example, don't say, "Why are you breastfeeding?" or "Why do you let them eat candy before dinner?" Again, not helpful. If you have real concerns, be careful to voice them in nonthreatening ways. You might say, "Sweetheart, perhaps the baby isn't getting satisfied with breast milk only, even though you are doing everything right. Maybe you should ask the doctor for suggestions." On the candy issue, it's better to let the mom figure that out on her own. (Some things aren't worth fighting for.)

2. Stop, Look, and Listen

This is an old rule that applies to many things, but for grandparents, if we will *stop* before jumping to conclusions, *look* to see exactly what is really happening, and *listen* for the motive behind the words being said, we will make better choices about what to say and when. Many methods for raising children have changed, and even if we had the latest, greatest everything during our child-rearing years, those things are obsolete. Baby cribs can't even have bumper pads anymore! What in the world? And your baby can't sleep on his stomach! Whoever heard of putting a baby on his back to sleep? So uncomfortable! And what is a baby sling? New items and techniques are just inventive ways of doing what moms and dads have always done—doing the best they can with what is available to them. Don't question what they think they need; don't criticize what they are doing or how they are doing it; don't critique the method they choose to incorporate. Stop, look, and listen to their new ways of doing things. You'll probably discover they are not that different after all.

3. Know Your Place

As the mother of two daughters, I am aware that I hold a special position. I knew that when my daughters went into marriage, they would most likely turn to me for help when problems arose. But because I have a son, I was also keenly aware of that same fact when he married. Daughters are more likely to turn to their mothers for help, and a daughter-in-law will turn to her own mother. If you have a son, don't be offended by this; it's just a reality. For all of us grandparents, we're the benchwarmers. The starting lineup is made up of Mom and Dad. The two sets of grandparents (or more in many cases) should be sitting on the sidelines waiting to get called into the game. Don't be offended when one gets called in before the other. Trust me—there will be plenty of opportunities, if you make yourself available, to get in the game.

My brother, who coached basketball for thirty years, always said, "You'll never play if you're not willing to sit on the bench." I recently met a proud grandma of nineteen-year-old twin grandsons. She claimed one as her own because when the babies were born, the first one was handed to the mommy and the second one was handed to her. Her daughter was already the mother of three when these twins were born. This grandma knew she was going to be needed. She and her husband moved immediately to the town where her daughter lived and assumed the position of benchwarmer. Trust me—they were both called into the game many times. Consequently, they have a very special relationship with all their grandchildren.

4. Keep the Peace

Many times when a baby is born, the happy occasion brings up old hurts. Divorce, stepfamilies, jealousy toward the family who lives closer to the baby, financial issues that might allow one family to give more expensive gifts—all these things can cause division in families at a time when peace and joy should be at the top of the list. The Bible tells us in Romans 12:18, "As far as it depends on you, live at peace with everyone" (NIV). I love this verse. We can't control what others say and do, but we can control what we say and do. My family relationships now include stepchildren, ex-wives, and ex-husbands. It's not where I envisioned my family to be, but it is where we are. The birth of a baby is only the first of many occasions that dictate that families be together—peacefully. Kindergarten graduations, dance recitals, football games, Grandparents Day celebrations, and on and on until college graduations. Interacting with "the other family" will forever be a part of life. As far as it depends on *you,* keep it peaceful.

It's important for children to see a family united not only during these happy milestones of their lives but also on a daily basis. It's hard, I know. It's hard to be nice when harsh things have been said and feelings have been hurt, but keep reminding yourself of Romans 12:18. If that doesn't work, remember the idiom that your grandmother used to say: "If you can't say anything nice, don't say anything at all." Say that over and over until you have it down.

And one more thing on this subject. Don't be quiet just to annoy or antagonize others. That's not keeping the peace. That type of passive-aggressive behavior is also not biblical. You can do this! After all, we're the peace-and-love generation, right?

5. You're Excused
Didn't you love it when your teacher said the words "You're excused"? That meant you could leave. Go. Get out of here. Those words are

music to the ears of every student. As grandparents, we have an enviable position. Unless you are raising your grandkids, you are *excused* from everything else. If things get a little testy while you're at the grandkids' house visiting, guess what—you can leave! You can write your own excuse. Isn't that the best? If you don't feel like going to another ball game, you don't have to. Seriously, we have the best job ever!

Back to the basketball analogy. If you're one of the starting five and you are sick, you're likely to play even if you have a temperature of 102 degrees. But if you're a benchwarmer and have a cold, stay home. No one really cares. As benchwarmers, our jobs are secure. Think about it like this: no one fights for the position of benchwarmer, but every coach needs one if one of the starting players gets hurt. So enjoy it. Be ready and willing to go in the game, but know you don't have to if you don't want to. You're excused.

Speak Up!

Earlier in this chapter, I confessed that I have a split personality on the issue of being silent. My shy self keeps me from speaking out around a crowd of folks I don't know, but my opinionated self allows me to use this "gift" on those close to me. Bless their hearts. (That's a southern saying for "I feel a little sorry for them.") There are certain things I will always speak up for or against. You're probably tired of my lists, but here's another one.

1. Rudeness/Bad Behavior

I do not allow children to be rude to me or anyone else while in my presence. I'm not saying it hasn't happened in my home, but if I'm around, I nip it in the bud. In modern America, we are all enjoying the benefits of feeling younger, dressing younger, and acting younger than grandparents of old, but we need to be careful that our newfound feeling of being younger doesn't encourage rude behavior from children who feel it is okay to take advantage of the situation. I've heard grandparents say, "I know he sounds rude, but it's just because he's comfortable around us. We're with him nearly every day. I guess you could say we're his best friends." *No!* Being with a child every day is not an excuse for bad behavior. And just as it wasn't good to be your child's best friend, it's not good to be your grandchild's best friend either, if that keeps you from expecting right behavior.

My mother, who is loved by all her grandchildren, is never afraid to put children in their place. In fact, one Christmas Eve we gave out awards for the year, and Mamaw Jo got the award for saying what everyone else was thinking. Mamaw Jo is never rude or mean, but she does expect right behavior.

We have a joke in our family now about good table manners. I always told my own children that it's important to have good table manners because one never knows when one might be invited to the White House for dinner. Of course, we never expected that to happen! But in 2015 Korie and Willie were invited to the White House Correspondents' Dinner. All my years of demanding good table manners paid off!

I can remember when my granddaughter Bella was around nine years old, she had a friend over to my house for lunch. Before we started eating, I said, "Please put your napkins in your laps." She leaned over to her friend and said, "At 2-mama's, you get lunch and a lesson on manners."

As adults, we have to set the expectations for good behavior. For some children, your home might be the only learning ground they have for good manners and respectful language. Don't run to the parents with a list of infractions when the children are in your home. Just handle it yourself. From the time they are little, speak confidently to them about how you expect them to act in your home, and they will figure it out. Let your children wonder why their children behave better for you than they do for them. It's one of the joys of being a grandparent!

All this holds true for bad behavior too. You know, the fussing and fighting that kids do. Trust me—just because you're the grandparent, you will not be exempt from listening to squabbling children. As grandparents, we know kids fight. We've lived through our own children fighting and treating one another as if they have cooties (remember that word?). But perhaps we're more patient and better equipped now. We can help our own children by reinforcing their rules and adding our own with our own twist. Be creative. Think of ways to get the point across that might be a different approach than their parents use.

Because my grands are often with me and because they are close in age, it was important that I establish rules for good behavior in my home and car. The car, as you know, can be a breeding ground for bickering. It's as if the minute the doors lock, the kids start arguing. Ugh! And there is nowhere for you to run and hide!

I remember one vacation to the beach when all my grandboys were around eight and nine years old. They filled the back seats of my van and truly were the best of friends—most of the time. But not that day. They seemed to argue about everything and pick on one another and annoy one another and on and on. Finally, I pulled the van over, unbuckled my seat belt, climbed into the back seat right in the middle of them, and started reading every Bible verse on treating others kindly. After about thirty minutes of reading, I ended with a short discussion on how God expects us to control our tongues and speak kindly to one another. The rest of the trip was pleasant, and I had to do that only once. They feared 2-mama climbing into the back seat from that day forward.

Be as creative as you can and want to be. Remember that the goal is raising children who speak kindly to one another, and your home and car will be peaceful most of the time. Realize they will grow up and out of that stage. (Praise the Lord!)

Now that all of mine are teenagers and older, they love one another and are great friends. After our trip to Israel, Sadie commented how much fun it was to get to know her cousin Maddox as a teenager. Maddox was fifteen at the time, and Sadie had not interacted with him as a teen very often. I loved hearing that. I loved seeing them tour Israel arm in arm, hand in hand. If your grands are in those squabbling years, take heart: this too shall pass.

2. Developmental Delays

This is a hard one. Many times parents are too close to the situation or not experienced enough to realize that there might be something wrong with their child. I have met many parents with only one child. It's hard to assess how a child is doing developmentally if you have no experience and no other child to compare her growth with. No parent wants to hear that a child isn't developing properly, but it's better for a grandparent, who loves the child as much as the parents do, to point out concerns than for the parents to hear it from another source.

As I have already mentioned, my background is education. I specifically taught children with learning disabilities, ranging from mild to severe. I have a brother who is severely dyslexic. Growing up, my siblings and I often helped my brother complete his homework and do other tasks he struggled with. Helping him was good training for my job and made me keenly aware of learning problems in others. If I notice a child who seems delayed in speech, motor skills, or social skills, I address it. You should too, but be careful and wise. Choose a time to speak up when the child is not present and you have time to listen to feedback. Make sure the parents are able to listen to your concerns without distractions, and be careful never to use words that sound accusatory. Developmental delays are no one's fault. They are in the wiring of particular children. Early intervention is the key.

> ★ ★ ★ ★
> ## Rockstar
> ### GRANDPARENTING
>
> What your children need more than advice and correction are love, affirmation, and cheerleading.

Speak up as soon as you feel something isn't right with the child. But keep in mind that the parents might not be willing to listen yet. If that is the case, back off. They will file away your concerns and come back to them when they are ready. It's important to realize the seriousness of this situation. Even suggesting something might be wrong with a child can be devastating. Be gentle and well informed. Don't speak up unless you feel confident there is a problem. Even as an educator, I wasn't in a position to diagnose children, but I was in a position to observe. As a grandparent, you are in the same position, especially if you are a caregiver for your grandchildren and have them on a daily basis. Still, it's a tough subject to approach.

Here are two things I learned as an educator and took into my grandparenting role:

1. Say something good and encouraging about the child first. "Teddy is the sweetest child. Today we were reading a book together and he held my hand as I read the entire book."

2. Share the concern as an observation, and include the parents. "Your father came in the room today, and the door slammed hard, but Teddy didn't react at all. Have you noticed that Teddy doesn't seem to hear loud noises?"

From there, hopefully a conversation can begin about getting the child the help he needs as soon as possible.

3. Dangerous Situations

This is another tough one. As your grands grow into late-elementary and teen years, you'll feel as if they live in danger mode. I want to scream "Wear a helmet!" nearly every day because several of mine live on the same street I live on. (I know—it's awesome!) I see them riding bikes, skateboards, and hoverboards (the ultimate dangerous moving vehicle) up and down the street. Fortunately, the street is relatively free of traffic because it's all families, but the riding toys are dangerous. I have to remind myself that my generation didn't wear helmets and survived childhood just fine.

Having said that, anytime you feel as if your grandchildren are in danger when they are in your care, you can play the "At this house, we don't do such and such" card. It's best not to hound the parents to buy helmets or watch the kids more diligently. Apparently they are comfortable with the level of protection they are providing, even if you're not.

But if you ever feel as though your grandchildren are in danger in a more serious way, such as abuse, you must speak up. This is the most difficult situation, but your grandchildren need you to be their advocate. If you notice unusual bruising, evidence of neglect, or personality changes in a grandchild, talk to one or both of the parents. Then if you don't get the answers you need, contact the authorities. This will be a very difficult decision, and if you have to do it, please know you are doing the right thing to protect your grandchild. I realize this means your own child (the parent of your grandchild) will feel as if you turned your back on her, but you must protect the young child. Steps to mend the adult/child relationship can happen later, after your grandchild is safely placed with either you or someone else.

You should never approach the parents about any conflicting ideals when your grandchildren are present. Children do not need to see adults discussing or disagreeing about concerns they have about the children. You never want to appear as if you don't trust the parents' decisions.

Ultimately, the care of your grandchildren is up to the parents. We should enjoy these years without having to make parenting decisions. Still, it's hard to keep our granny mouths shut when we think a haircut is in order or the dresses our teen granddaughters are wearing are too short. It's true that we're older, wiser, and more experienced, but as our moms used to say to us, "Zip it." Our opinion on most subjects will not be welcomed or warranted and will generally be winked at by our adult kids.

Okay, reader, let's both take the sound of silence pledge:

I promise to be a part of my grandkids' lives without offering uninvited parenting tips to their parents, who are capable, loving adults.

———

A truly wise person uses few words;
    a person with understanding is even-tempered.
Even fools are thought wise when they keep silent;
    with their mouths shut, they seem intelligent.

—Proverbs 17:27–28

Let It Be

*W*hen Philip was in seventh grade, his mother and father went through a terrible divorce. Even as a seventh grader, Philip knew that both parents had done things they shouldn't have done. Philip was understandably hurt by their choices. He took a path he shouldn't have taken and spent the next fifteen years running from his problems. Alcohol, drugs, and partying were a constant in his life until he met Carrie. Carrie had also struggled her way through her teens and early twenties, but she finally found her way out and was drug- and alcohol-free when she met Philip. After a two-year engagement, Philip and Carrie married. They recently had their first baby, a boy. Philip watches his parents and their new spouses dote on the new baby. That little boy is surrounded by love, but Philip is left to deal with his mixed feelings of rejection and love from his own childhood.

Carolyn's single mother, Jan, wasn't a faithful believer in Jesus when Carolyn was a child. Carolyn often felt neglected because her mom spent more hours at work and on dates than she did at home. Carolyn was a latchkey kid who, beginning in third grade, let herself into the house every afternoon after school. When Carolyn was in tenth grade, her mom attended church with a friend and came to know Jesus. She began to make better choices and spent more time with Carolyn. Still, Carolyn remembers the lonely hours. Carolyn met Jim during her junior year of college. They married after graduation and are now the proud parents of two little boys. Carolyn looks at her boys and wonders how her mom could have left her alone for much of her life. Still, she's happy her mom is here for her now.

Jennifer's dad was described as strict by her friends. He set the standard high for his children and expected them to reach that standard. Jennifer worried about her grades, her friends, her activities, and her choices because she wanted to please her dad. One of her siblings went a different route. He gave up pleasing his dad and chose to rebel instead. Jennifer's mom tried to keep the peace, to add some balance and order to the home, but Jennifer's dad's personality was stronger by a long shot. He wasn't ever abusive—not even close. It was just hard to get along with him and measure up to his expectations. Jennifer met Colin on a double date. He was dating her best friend. After her best friend and Colin broke up, Jennifer and Colin discovered they had a lot in common. They dated, got married, and are now the parents of one boy and two girls. Jennifer smiles when she watches her dad play with her kids and wonders why she didn't have "that dad"—the dad she now sees he could have been.

Life is tough. Unfortunately, making bad choices doesn't stop once we become parents. Our adult years are not spent excused from making wrong decisions. I wish they were. Life would be much easier if, at twenty-one, we were suddenly as wise as the proverbial owl, but that's not how it goes. If you were like me, you spent at least a few nights a week lying in bed worrying whether what you said or did that day would affect your child forever in a negative way.

Some mistakes are small, such as punishing the wrong child after a fight breaks out at the dinner table; others are big, such as having an affair or committing a crime. I know those are biggies, for sure, but they happen every day. My husband and I considered ourselves to be good parents, but we still made mistakes. My parents considered themselves to be good parents, but they made mistakes. Their parents were good parents, but they made mistakes. We all do.

Our tempers flare; our selfishness overtakes us; our own sadness or disappointments consume us; our fears deceive us. All these things and more keep us from being the mistake-free adults we want to be. The Bible is full of people who made mistakes. I'm convinced God was deliberate in His decision to raise up the likes of Peter, who denied knowing Jesus; and Paul, who persecuted Christians; and Moses, who disobeyed God and struck a very important rock. I think God wants us to never grow comfortable with our mistakes but to acknowledge them and grow past them.

Whether you made a bad decision or straight-up sinned, God can and will bring you through it. Romans 8:1–2 are two of my favorite verses: "There is no condemnation for those who belong to Christ Jesus. And because you belong to him, the power of the life-giving Spirit has freed you from the power of sin that leads to death."

Once we declare our love and loyalty to Jesus Christ, we are free from the power of sin. What a glorious thing it is to realize that all our past mistakes are washed away by the blood of Jesus. But here's the deal with sin. I learned this valuable statement from a youth minister I once worked with. He often told the teenagers who were in our care, "When you're through with sin, it's not through with you." That means once you're done with the ultimate penalty of sin, its consequences don't go away. God will forgive you, and people will forgive you, but you will still pay the price. The teen who finds herself pregnant and not married can be forgiven, but who will ultimately care for her child? The young man who drinks too much and wrecks his parents' car can be forgiven, but he is still responsible for the damage done. The dad who has an affair and destroys his family can be forgiven, but he still has to live with the consequences of his poor choices.

One of the great things about aging is that a certain amount of maturity is bound to happen. All the mistakes we make teach us something; in fact, they teach us a lot, and hopefully we become wiser. But a mistake or sin might cause issues with your children well into their adulthood. How can you move past them? How can you spend your grandparenting years free from the shame of poor decisions made earlier in life?

Cue the song choice for this chapter: "When I find myself in times of trouble . . ."[1] This Beatles song was released in 1970 as the title song of the album. It is the number one song in the "Fans' Top 10" poll in *100 Best Beatles Songs: A Passionate Fan's Guide* by Stephen J. Spignesi and Michael Lewis.[2] It's easy to see why, isn't it? Has there ever been a more comforting song than "Let It Be"? It has been covered by many artists, including these greats: Aretha Franklin, Jennifer Hudson, and Ray Charles. If I could sing, I would definitely cover this song, but that's another story.

At a recent Paul McCartney concert I attended, it was as if the entire audience was waiting for this song to be played. The applause was nearly deafening as Sir Paul took to the piano for the beautiful introduction of "Let It Be." Even with all the noise, there was a calm and comforting spirit that overtook the room as Paul sang the words so familiar to everyone in the audience.

This song resonates with many as we all search for a way to "let things be" or let go of the things in the world that distract us, bring us pain, and cause us to get stuck in our shame. In researching these lyrics, I discovered the root of the song isn't what I thought it was. Maybe, like me, you thought the song was evoking the aid of Mary, the mother of Jesus, to help in troubled times. That is certainly a logical assumption. But it's not the truth. It seems Paul was in a very dark time of his life. He was partying too much, doing drugs, and not getting much sleep. (Hmm . . . imagine that of a '60s rocker.) One night he went to sleep particularly anxious and worried. He dreamed of his mother, who had died when he was fourteen years old. Her name was Mary. McCartney described his mother, saying,

> She had been a nurse, my mum, and very hardworking, because she wanted the best for us. We weren't a well-off family—we didn't have a car, we just about had a television—so both of my parents went out to work, and Mum contributed a good half to the family income. At night when she came home, she would cook, so we didn't have a lot of time with each other. But she was just a very comforting presence in my life. And when she died, one of the difficulties I had, as the years went by, was that I couldn't recall her face so easily. That's how it is for everyone,

I think. As each day goes by, you just can't bring their face into your mind, you have to use photographs and reminders like that.

In his dream, his mother came to him, and he could see her face clearly as she comforted him and told him to "let it be."[3]

Wow! I didn't see that coming! It's no wonder this song is special. I wish I had known these facts before I saw Paul McCartney in concert.

Letting things be might be the single most difficult task we humans have. God gave us a memory, and what a blessing it is. My grandmother died of complications from Alzheimer's disease. The saddest part of Alzheimer's is that life, through memories, is taken away. Each time we visited my grandmother, it seemed more of her life story was gone. It wasn't really gone; others could tell the story, but she couldn't. She simply had no memory of it.

Memory is a fickle friend, isn't it? When we want to see our adult children as babies, we can close our eyes and remember the giggles, the tiny feet, and the little curl of hair. But that same memory also files away our bad choices. We close our eyes, and we're back to the fight we had with our teen about a party he wanted to attend. Our memories cause us to hang on to negative comments from others and our own bad decisions for longer than we should. Yes, memory is both our friend and our foe.

I love the Olympics. In 2006 I was glued to the television any time I had a chance, watching the winter competition. One evening I was watching two Chinese skaters—Zhang Dan and her partner, Zhang Hao—compete for a gold medal. Little did I know I was about to learn a valuable life lesson from their performance. Oh, how graceful these two were as they glided across the ice with such ease. Then the announcer said they were going to attempt a never-before-landed quadruple salchow. I had no idea what that was, but I knew it was going to be quite heroic. I did know that *quadruple* meant "four," so four of something was going to take place, and their dreams of Olympic gold would surely come true. As Zhang Hao threw his beautiful partner into the air, she went spinning like a colorful top. It seemed everyone watching collectively held his or her breath to see whether she could stick the landing, but it was not to be. As she landed, her ankle gave way and Zhang Dan hit the ice hard. She slid until she crashed into the retaining wall. At the time I called it "the thud heard around the world." Cameras shot to her teammates, who stood with their hands over their mouths and their eyes filling with tears, then to the crowd of Olympic fans, each staring in disbelief and horror. In homes around the world, millions of viewers like me watched from our living rooms, too shocked to speak. But the real story was still to come.

Zhang Dan slowly and carefully skated to the side as she rubbed her knees and cried. Her partner was right beside her, comforting her and holding her up. Everyone assumed they were finished, their Olympic dream over. But after less than five minutes, as if by some predetermined cue, the pair proudly skated out to resume their routine at the precise moment the fall had interrupted it. In an interview, Zhang Dan stated, "We didn't say any words of giving up. We are at the Olympics." Wow! Such courage from someone so young! The pair received the silver medal that year, but in the hearts of fans around the world, their performance was gold.

Life will deliver some pretty tough blows. By our grandparenting years, many mistakes have been made, many walls have been hit, many bumps and bruises have been bandaged, leaving us feeling inadequate and unworthy. From these two skaters, I learned that getting up when you're knocked to the ground might be hard but it's always possible. And I love Zhang Dan's reasoning. She simply said, "We are at the Olympics." In other words, they were at the top, the peak, the highest point of the mountain. Nothing was going to stop them from competing.

As believers, that's how we should live every day. We should know that life with God is the highest place we will ever be and, even with bumps and bruises, it's worth it to get up and keep going.

Zephaniah 3:17 says this about our Father in heaven:

The LORD your God is living among you. (He is present.)
>   He is a mighty savior. (He is strong.)
He will take delight in you with gladness. (He enjoys you.)
>   With his love, he will calm all your fears. (He loves you and
>   is there to calm you.)
>   He will rejoice over you with joyful songs. (He sings over
>   you.) [Commentary in parentheses is mine.]

I love that last phrase. Close your eyes for a minute and imagine God singing over you. Whose voice do you imagine? Paul McCartney's? Percy Sledge's? Elvis Presley's? Adele's? These people are definitely great singers. But God's voice? I imagine it will be a voice like none we've ever known. On those days when you feel as though you have hit the ground with both knees and you do not know whether you can go on, be still and listen to the music God is singing over you.

There are steps Zhang Dan or any athlete has to take to get back in the game after an injury or setback. There might be some steps you need to take to let the past be. Here are a few that might help you on your journey.

Right the Wrong

In any recovery program, one of the steps is to apologize to those you have offended. It's a hard step because it involves leaving yourself open to more criticism and shame. But the opposite usually occurs. Generally, such encounters result in forgiveness, which is the purpose. I'm not saying you should apologize to your child for making her mad at the dinner table when she refused to eat carrots in the fifth grade. I'm talking about the major mistakes you know have caused pain to your family. If you have done something to harm your family, own up to it. Don't spend the rest of your life with an elephant in the room. Get it out in the open. Apologize. Then you can start to heal and move forward in your relationships.

Grandchildren are remarkable family bonders. Bringing a new baby into the family is like a big glob of superglue. Mom, Dad, grandpas, grandmas, cousins, uncles, brothers, sisters—everyone is now bound together by something smaller than a bread box. And the door is open for forgiveness. Everyone is eager to bring nothing but love and good feelings to this new family member. It might be uncomfortable for a few minutes the first time you are all together, but you can do it. I'll borrow a phrase I learned from my granddaughter Sadie. It's "five seconds of awkward." She says five seconds of awkward is better than a lifetime of regret. You can apply this principle to many areas. Be willing to be awkward for five seconds so your family can spend the rest of their lives together in peace.

If you choose (which you should) to apologize for past wrongs, consider the timing very carefully. Don't do it right before the gender-reveal party. Don't do it in the hospital room prior to delivery. Don't do it while your sweet daughter or daughter-in-law is recovering at home. Choose a time when you have enough time to talk the situation over with no distractions. Or you could opt to write a letter. Writing it down is often the best choice because it gives you an opportunity to word your letter carefully and allows the person you are writing to the time needed to absorb the information he or she has been given.

Let's follow the example of our skater Zhang Dan, who skated even though she was injured. Moving on in life often involves pushing through even when pain is present. As I said earlier, being forgiven of a sin doesn't mean the consequences will magically go away, but admitting it is the first step to moving past it.

Don't Hang Out at Your Own Pity Party

It's easy to feel sorry for ourselves. After all, it was our life, our mistake. But don't do it. Dwelling on your mistakes will not benefit anyone. It will leave you feeling depressed and helpless. Take your mind off the past by making your present more interesting. Get lost in helping others. Join a gym. Work out. Get in better shape. Take a class at the local college. Do whatever is needed to take your mind off yourself and focus on something more productive. Give yourself permission to let it be. Recovering from a mistake takes time. As more time passes, you will see that others have moved on, so you can too. Most people are too busy recovering from their own issues to dwell on yours. Don't invite yourself to your own pity party. Focus on something that brings joy and hope and love to others.

Don't Waste It

Rick Warren has often said, "Don't waste your pain." Even the preacher of a megachurch is not free from the pain this life can bring. He speaks from his own life experiences, one of them being the suicide of his son. While much of the pain we encounter in life is of our own doing, some is inflicted on us by others. In any case, Rick Warren's words ring true: don't waste your pain. Use whatever you have gone through to help someone else.

My husband is a colon cancer survivor. He lives with a colostomy. He has never felt sorry for himself; rather, he considers himself blessed to be cancer-free for more than twenty years. He spends hours helping other colon cancer patients. Rick Warren said in his book *The Purpose Driven Life,* "Your greatest life messages and your most effective ministry will come out of your deepest hurts."[4] When my husband heard the devastating diagnosis of colon cancer, his first thought certainly wasn't how helpful he could be to others. His first thought was *How can I get well?* Doctors were called. Appointments were made. Treatments were scheduled. It was a whirlwind of chemo, radiation, and surgery. But once he had walked through it, his very next thought was *How can I help others?* He knew he didn't want to waste the pain he had been through.

Some of our dearest friends are Alan and Lisa Robertson. They now spend most of their time traveling around the country speaking to couples about forgiveness and faith in a marriage. They are not trained marriage therapists. They are two people who made a ton of mistakes but turned their lives around, and now their mistakes are the backdrop for their amazing message of hope and forgiveness. I remember the phone call I got from Alan telling me that his marriage to Lisa was over. He was crushed and didn't know how his life would go on. Honestly, at that moment, I didn't either. But "with God all things are possible" (Matthew 19:26, NIV). Alan and Lisa tell their story of how poor decisions, shame, and regret nearly destroyed their marriage in their book, *A New Season*. These two people choose to live honestly in front of the world, and in doing so, they help others going through similar challenges. Don't waste your pain. Consider using whatever difficult time you have been through to guide someone else. Your healing will come sooner rather than later when you focus on others' needs instead of your own shame.

I'm going to be dead honest here. I was the good kid growing up. I don't think it's because I was born to be good. More likely, I was born shy and afraid, and fear sometimes makes you good. I was afraid to be bad. I was scared of my teachers, definitely afraid of the principal, afraid of the babysitter, scared I would hurt my parents' feelings, and afraid I might make my siblings mad. Basically, I was afraid of everything.

As I matured and studied the Bible more closely, I began to see scriptures about being bold and confident in God. I made a decision to walk not in fear but in boldness. Fortunately for me, my "journey to a bolder me" started in my late twenties, after I married and had children.

Maybe if I hadn't been a scaredy-cat, I would have dabbled in drinking or drugs or cigarettes. I hope not. I like to think that fear wasn't my only motivator, but I have to admit that it played a huge part. Perhaps that isn't all bad. The Bible tells us in Proverbs 10:27 that the fear of the Lord leads to long life.

In the early 1990s, when church conferences for ladies became all the rage, I loved attending and listening to the life stories of many amazing women around the country. After listening to the speakers at some of these events, I began to question how my "good kid" status could be used in ministry. I began to ask myself, *What do I have to offer others? What is my testimony? What stories do "good" kids tell? If Rick Warren is right when he says, "Your greatest life messages and your most effective ministry will come out of your deepest hurts," how will I have an effective ministry?*

This puzzled me for the longest time. Then I realized that not only had I been born with a "scared" gene but I had also been blessed with parents who taught me how to cope with disappointments in life. My siblings and I were taught not to wring our hands but to face problems head-on. I came to understand that I had been through some hard things, but I was taught how to deal with them.

At some point in my twenties, I took an inventory of my life and discovered I had been through some pretty hard things. Things like being bullied, having friends who got involved in bad behavior, moving to another state at a young age, witnessing a sister who was run over by a car, and experiencing the devastation of a beloved aunt choosing to divorce my uncle and leave her family. I began to see that life will have its ups and downs and that it's in those down moments that we get to choose how we will react and whom we will cling to. I learned, by example, to stand strong and cling to God.

As time has gone on, more of the "biggies" that happen in life have happened to me. In my late twenties, when my children were young, I suffered a life-threatening illness. My husband's mother struggled with a mental illness all her life. My husband battled colon cancer at age forty-eight. We lost three of our parents in a five-year span. Two of our children have been through divorces. Of course, I am naming just a few. By the time anyone reaches her midsixties, an assortment of "biggies" have

Rockstar GRANDPARENTING

One of the great things about aging is that a certain amount of maturity is bound to happen.

most likely occurred. Take all those "biggies" and use them as stepping-stones to a stronger faith. Don't pile one on top of another to hold you down from living the life God has planned for your later years. Accept where you are. Accepting brings immediate relief. Don't make any one mistake—no matter how big—a defining moment.

When the song "One Moment in Time" came out, I immediately loved it. I know it's not one of our rocker hits, but it's a good song with lyrics that make you want to jump higher, run faster, sing louder . . . you get the message. Anyway, one of the lines says, "I want one moment in time when I'm more than I thought I could be."[5] When I first heard that song, I was like "Yes, that's what I want!" One moment "when I'm racing with destiny," striving to be the very best at something significant. (Okay, I'm easily influenced by music.) But the truth is, I want lots of "moments in time" when I'm more than I thought I could be. I want to wake up and cook today's pancake better than yesterday's pancake. I want my grandkids to think I can do anything. I want my husband to be proud he chose me. I want my children to be inspired by me. I want to live in search of the next defining moment, not reliving the last one.

Don't let yesterday's bad decisions keep you from being the very best you tomorrow. Remember how I said your grandchildren will see only the end of your life. They have missed the mistakes, the bad decisions, the poor choices—they have you only today. Let the past be and get on with a great today and tomorrow.

———

No, dear brothers and sisters, I have not achieved it, but I focus on this one thing: *Forgetting* the past and looking forward to what lies ahead.

—Philippians 3:13

Wish I Was a Kellogg's Cornflake

*W*hen I first heard the words "Wish I was a Kellogg's corn-flake," I was sitting in chemistry class in eleventh grade. Chemistry was a drag, but that song was outta sight! (How's that for remembering some boomer slang?) Now, you're probably wondering how in the world I heard a song in chemistry class, because goodness knows there was no easy way to play music while we were in school. No cell phones, no iPods, no computers—nothing! Taking a record player or transistor radio to school was definitely a rad idea, but the detention that followed would have been a bummer.

Here's how I heard the lyrics. I had two guy friends who mastered every Simon & Garfunkel song within hours of it hitting the radio. They were seriously cool! Just like this simple yet multifaceted tune. I had no idea that masked by the clever lyrics about cereal and muffins were undertones of dodging the Vietnam War—or at least that's what many deeper-than-I-am thinkers have said. To me, it was just a fun song with a light beat, tight harmonies, and lyrics that made me think. (Now I sound like a contestant on *American Bandstand*.)

I didn't want to be a Kellogg's cornflake or an English muffin, but the song challenged me to think about what life would be like if I was one, and in doing that, it challenged me to think of what I really did want out of life. I imagined "floatin' in my bowl, takin' movies, relaxin' awhile, livin' in style,"[1] and realized that anything was possible.

Whether it's dreaming of life as a cornflake or a doctor or a teacher or a writer or just dreaming about doing nothing, dreaming is a part of life for the young. And it should be. After all, they still have a lot of days left, while our days are now fewer. Hopefully you've lived your dreams and are now entering your grandparenting years feeling fulfilled in many areas. But life is not over, and we should not view it as such. Whatever number of years you have left is time enough to set new goals, reach new heights, and explore new adventures.

We have two big jobs as grandparents. We talked a little about this in chapter 5. One is being a teacher and the other is being a student. Both are important to foster a great relationship with our grand-children. I will never forget my four-year-old Bella (who's sixteen now) teaching me how to use a cell phone. She said, "2-mama, you need to get some apps." To which I replied at the time, "What's an app?" I had a lot to learn and I still do. Each of my grandchildren has been called on to teach me the latest techy information about Snapchat, Instagram, Poshmark, Twitter, Musical.ly—you get the picture. It seems that just as I learn about the next greatest thing, another great thing comes out and I have to depend on a child to show me the way. And that's a good thing. It gives me a chance to interact with my grandchildren in an area where they excel.

But no relationship is one sided. What are your grands learning from you? Grandparents are the perfect choice for showing children what the expression "Broaden your horizon" means. Let's face it—our grandchildren are living in a tiny box with a screen that supplies friends and fake adventures but little real-life experience. They need us to be the hands and feet of life outside a box. We need to show them what life is like when they put the phone down and do . . . anything. And it's fun to keep them guessing about the talents we have acquired over the years. One day in church, two of my grands were using sign language to communicate with each other. My best friend growing up had a grandmother who was deaf. I learned sign language so we could do exactly what my granddaughters were doing. But my grands didn't know this . . . until I reached over and signed, "What are you two doing?" They both looked at me with huge eyes and signed, "Did you read our sign language?" I just shrugged and went back to listening to the preacher. Yes, it's best to keep them guessing and pull out your best talents when necessity calls for them.

It's also important to include our grands in the things we do and value. I have loved taking our grandkids on mission trips. I started this when John Luke was twelve years old. Our home church began a new ministry in the Dominican Republic. I decided to take John Luke with me that first year. It was new to both of us. We had no idea what to expect, but we faced it together. To this day, we smile when we see a can of Pringles because we discovered them that first year in a little store in the village of Neyba. You would have thought we found gold! Taking John Luke on that mission trip was one of the best decisions I have ever made. Over the years, as the kids got older, I added more of my grands to the trip. For several summers now, my two daughters and most of my grands, as well as several teens from our home church, have made the trip with me. Because of that work, my grandchildren are well aware of the plight of those less fortunate in our world. We are blessed to live in America and I am thankful for the opportunities being born in America brings our family, but I want my kids and grandkids to be appreciative of what they have and to be sensitive to the needs of others.

Johnny's mom, Mamaw Howard, didn't take her grands on mission trips. In fact, she had a fear of flying, but every Wednesday morning she baked cookies, picked up her grands, and headed to a nursing home to minister to the men and women there. You see, you don't have to go far to broaden the horizons of children. Chances are whatever you do will be new to them and will teach them valuable life lessons.

I get it. Grandparents, we are busy too. Many of us are already car pool drivers, ball game attendees, homework helpers, moneylenders, and date night babysitters. Most of us are already more involved with our grandchildren than our grandparents ever dreamed of. This section isn't just about us doing more with our grandkids; it's about us doing more for ourselves. And in doing more for ourselves, we show our grandkids that life doesn't stop at fifty or sixty or seventy or eighty. When I was asked to be a part of the mission effort to the Dominican Republic, I wasn't just thinking about John Luke. I was thinking about myself too. I needed to go to the mission field. I needed to grow in areas I had not grown in.

I started playing tennis at the age of forty-two. At the time, and more so now, I didn't think forty-two was old. However, there were some telltale signs that I wasn't young anymore. For instance, I went to the doctor for a sinus infection and read my chart that described me as a middle-aged woman. *What?* If I could have found an eraser, that description might have conveniently disappeared. (In other words, apparently I wasn't going to handle aging well! If you're wondering whether you're middle aged, one dictionary states it's between the ages of forty-five and sixty-five, but you can decide.) Okay, back to tennis. I had always wanted to play tennis but never found the time. At forty-two I had what I considered a little free time. Even though I worked full time, my kids were either married or in college. I had one grandbaby due later that year, but the window of opportunity for some free time was open.

At my first lesson, I noticed I was the oldest in my group. Most of the women were fifteen to twenty years younger than me. But I was not deterred, and now I'm a pretty decent tennis player with over twenty years' experience. I have knowledge of a lifetime sport that I enjoy with my kids and grandkids (and I often beat them). Over the years I've played on a few teams that have done well, and I even made it to nationals a few years back. On that team, my daughter Ashley was our youngest teammate, and I was the oldest. It was fun! The grands rarely come to watch me play (apparently the watching thing isn't reciprocated), but they all know 2-mama is a tennis player. It's okay that they don't watch me play. I play for myself, even though I love that I'm teaching my grandkids an important life lesson along the way. What is that lesson? I'm not sure whether my grands think it's cool that I play tennis. I'm guessing they don't think much about it, just as I didn't think much about what my grandparents did with their lives, but I like to think my tennis playing tells them to follow their dreams, no matter how old they are. Perhaps it's a subtle message, but it's out there for them to receive.

As I said, for the most part, grandparents have more time than parents do, and hopefully the grandparenting years bring a time when finances are more dependable. Still, finding the time and energy to be all we want to be can be challenging. Like many of you, I worked full time until my grandchildren were in upper elementary school and older. Yes, I had days of extreme guilt because I wasn't the one taking care of them when their mom and dad were busy, but I got over it . . . sort of.

When John Luke and Sadie were born, I was still teaching school. I loved for them to visit me at school. When they were just toddlers, I left teaching and joined my husband as we built a publishing company. My grands used to love to come see me at work and get candy from the candy drawer. When they left, I would take a moment to mentally regroup and then would go back to work. In a nine-year span, ten grandchildren were born. John Luke and Sadie were alone for only two years, and then we added two babies a year until Aevin, our youngest, was born in 2004.

Those were crazy years of juggling my work schedule and helping my daughters and daughter-in-law with little ones. I remember one time I was keeping all the kids while the parents had a weekend away. On Saturday morning, I came down with a stomach virus. I spent the entire day on the couch while little bodies rolled over me. Toys covered the floor of our playroom. But looking back, I wouldn't trade getting to be a part of my grandkids' lives for anything.

For many, the choice to stop working and help with the grandchildren is the right choice. For others, there is no choice. They have to continue working to support themselves. Don't feel as though you have to be a stay-at-home grandparent to have a relationship with your grands. The fact that you have a job teaches your grands the importance of working hard and gives them another view of the world. Explain to them what your job is and why it's important for you to be there.

When Sadie was little, she hated when I traveled for work, which was often. I can remember her coming over (we live next door) and asking why I had to leave again. I would explain to her what my job involved and tell her I loved her and would be back soon. Obviously, she got the message because now she travels all over the country and I want her to stay home! Our roles have reversed, but I am tremendously proud of her and her desire to share the message of Jesus with young people around the world. I like to think the lifestyle she saw her grandparents live out helped her decide to follow her dreams.

For the last eight years, I have been more of a stay-at-home grandma, but I have also written eight books, hosted a weekly radio show, started a grandma T-shirt line, tutored kids, and directed a summer camp, as well as attended nearly every possible grandkid event on the calendar. Still, I don't go to an office every day. My thirteen-year-old grandson, Aevin, recently asked me whether I was retired. I said I wasn't really because I still have many jobs. They just don't require me to go to an office. He thought for a minute and then said, "I'm just going to say you're retired, because you stay home to work." Okay, that seemed to work for him.

I love being able to set my own schedule and be available to go to school to eat lunch with the grands or take them to the doctor if they're sick or join them on a field trip. All that is awesome, but if I have a book deadline to meet, I have to decline the offers and stay home and work. They are used to that as well. We might not like it, but it's what life is about. It's about working and playing and finding time when it doesn't seem available and understanding when there isn't enough time and giving everyone grace when it's needed.

Thomas Jefferson is quoted as saying, "If you want something you've never had, you have to be willing to do something you've never done." I love that! This life is full of new adventures and crazy ideas and fun experiences and remarkable opportunities, but we have to take the first step toward embracing them. I love new beginnings. I love every New Year because I love New Year's resolutions. I'm a list maker and list checker-off-er (another word that's not a word). I love to accomplish new things and then take them off the list and go to the next thing. If you feel as though you're stuck in a grandparenting rut, it's time to dig out of the rut and make a checklist of new adventures. Whatever it is that you're feeling passionate about, start now. Your next twenty years will not go any slower than the previous twenty, so here's my advice: Don't delay. Sign up today for anything you want to do!

Here are a few things you can do to be intentional about showing your grandkids that old dogs can learn new tricks.

Remind Yourself That Learning Something New Is Fun

It's possible that the years of "doing stuff" have left you with the feeling that you're done and you may not want to do anything else in life. But wait! Think back to that first bicycle ride or the first time you drove a car or jumped off a diving board. It was fun, wasn't it? Don't let the youngsters have all the fun in life; you should get in on some of it too. I continue to take tennis lessons with my kids and grandkids. We all love learning new skills together and practicing our skills and laughing about how bad we are. It's just fun. Your choice doesn't have to be a sport or something rigorous. There are plenty of new things to see and do without sweating. My eighty-four-year-old uncle just wrote a novel. No one knew he even had a desire or the skill to write a novel until he handed it to us. Before that, he decided to make decorative birdhouses. He's an inspiration to our family by quietly starting something new. It's clear he doesn't do what he does for anyone else but simply enjoys challenging himself to new adventures.

Start an Old Activity Again

Look back at your life and think about the things that brought you joy. Pick one of those activities and begin it again. You'll be surprised at how much you remember and how quickly you pick it back up. My husband played in a rock band during his teen years. Our grandkids didn't know that until a few years ago when the band decided it was time for a reunion. Out came the guitar, and 2-papa was eighteen again, playing bass guitar and harmonizing with three old friends. It was fun to watch our grandkids' faces as they sat in awe of their grandpa and his talents. Maybe there's a sport you used to play or a musical instrument you need to dust off or you used to love to sew and always wanted to re-cover a couch. Whatever it is that at one time brought you joy still can. These are the things that make connecting with this generation easy. It turns out several of our grandkids are musically inclined, and they love talking music with 2-papa. Some of the time, they even think he's pretty cool.

Start Something Completely New

Our brains love to learn new information. Now is the perfect time to ask yourself what it is that you always wanted to do but didn't have time. Perhaps you always wanted to go on a mission trip, learn a new language, make your own dress, cook a fancy meal, decorate a cake, give a speech, jump out of an airplane, travel to China, or wrestle an alligator (just kidding . . . making sure you were paying attention). There is an endless list of things you and I haven't done. The brain is amazingly complex, and even the greatest scientists don't totally understand it. In fact, when I googled the word *brain,* over a billion results popped up. A billion!

Don't you love Google? No more *World Book* encyclopedias taking up space on our bookshelves! And speaking of Google, or maybe I should say YouTube, the internet is a great way to learn new things. My grandson Asa has never taken a piano lesson, yet he plays beautifully. He taught himself using YouTube videos—and practice, of course. What an exciting time we live in! I've taught myself a few things by googling or finding them on YouTube, including how to make a T-shirt quilt for John Luke for Christmas one year and how to play the ukulele. You may have talents you didn't even know you had!

Change Something You Do
on a Regular Basis

Research shows that doing something as small as brushing our teeth with the opposite hand is good for brain development. Make a pledge to continue to learn new things just by doing things differently. Take a look at your habits, such as where you sit at the dinner table or what side of the bed you sleep on (now I'm stepping on toes, right?). Seriously, just by changing one habit, you will open the door to trying new things. It will make you feel a little rebellious inside, not in a bad 1960s kind of way, but in a way that makes life seem more exciting.

My sweet mom is determined not to fall into the "old person" trap of doing the same thing every day. We laugh at her, but she has a point. As I mentioned earlier, my mom took care of three of my grandparents at one time. She knows all about old people and their attachment to the same daily activities. My Grandma Shack loved to watch her "stories," or soap operas, in the afternoons. When Grandma had control of the television, no one need ask whether the channel could be changed. That wasn't hap-

Rockstar GRANDPARENTING

Whether you are young or old, the grandkids won't notice your age. They only know you now and how much you love them.

pening. My daddy loved to tease her and walk in front of the TV or threaten to change the channel, just to "ruffle her feathers," he would say. Even at eighty-seven, my mom shies away from anything that even hints at being a daily old-person habit. She's even reluctant to meet her granddaughter and her family at Cracker Barrel every Saturday morning for breakfast just because it "sounds old." But she does it because it's valuable time with the great-grandkids. In this case, Mom submitted to a new habit to enjoy her family more. Mom learned that not all habits mean you're old; some new habits are actually good choices that bring great joy. Now on Saturday mornings she might be challenged by her five-year-old great-grandson to a game of checkers or talked into buying a treat for the three-year-old (who could resist?), and she doesn't regret doing the same thing every Saturday.

We all love the things that make us feel comfortable and safe, and of course, there is nothing wrong with that. But if you're someone who wants to keep life exciting, just change a few things and see how differently you think and act.

My husband and I have over twenty years of experience being grandparents. Just like our parenting years, each stage of life with our grandchildren has brought a new set of challenges as well as adventures. We were blessed to be a young grandma and grandpa when our grandchildren were toddlers. We could run and play and stay up late as if they were our own babies. Being a young grandparent gives you more energy but less time because you're usually still employed full time and active in church and community events. Being an older grandparent might afford you more time but less energy. I'm here to tell you whether you are young or old, the grandkids won't notice your age. They know you only as you are now and how much you love them.

———

Plant your seed in the morning and keep busy all afternoon, for you don't know if profit will come from one activity or another—or maybe both.

—ECCLESIASTES 11:6

I Got You Babe

When John Luke was born, I announced to my husband that I was in love with another man and he weighed around eight pounds. If a heart could burst and throw confetti all around the room, my heart, on October 11, 1995, would have done that. I tell my friends they should be very happy that social media didn't exist when John Luke was born. Picture overload would have taken on a new meaning because he was seriously the cutest kid ever. Praise the Lord I didn't have to put my friends and family through that! I loved that baby boy with all my being, and then my love multiplied over and over again as each grandchild took his or her place in my heart.

But here's the reality: even the most loving, adoring grandchildren will grow up and leave the ever-ready-to-hold lap of a devoted grandmother. There was a time when John Luke was my shadow, following me around like an obedient puppy. But that was then and this is now. He had the nerve to get married *and* move away all in one year and at the young age of nineteen! Obviously, our love affair was one sided! Alas, each of our precious grands will do the same, and once again, our house will be quiet and 2-papa will be overjoyed that he can run around in his underwear again. Nobody warned me that I would experience an empty nest twice in my life.

Johnny and I have always loved this famous Sonny & Cher song because it's a small reflection of our life and marriage right down to the line that talks about his hair being too long. (Johnny had the coolest long hair ever!) When this song hit the charts in 1965, I have no doubt moms and dads all over the world rolled their eyes at the recklessness of the lyrics. "They say we're young and we don't know . . ."[1] "Exactly!" screamed the parents of hopeful young loves seeking a thumbs-up from their parents. The young loves collectively thanked Sonny & Cher for giving them permission to marry even though they couldn't pay the rent. (A minor thing, really.) Sonny & Cher were handed over to exasperated parents as exhibit number one when their kids boldly declared there was no mountain they couldn't climb.

Oh, to be young and full of hope again. Or not! Now, as grandparents, we see the reality that goes along with being young and full of hope but short of nearly everything else. A good job, money in the bank, a decent set of communication skills—these things come only with time and hard work. And we were not an exception to any of this. Contrary to the popular belief of my grandkids, who think everyone married young in the 1970s, being married at eighteen and twenty was considered very young even in 1971. The average age at that time was around twenty-one for women and twenty-three for men.[2] Most of our friends were not married during our early married life. When I was home washing dishes, my friends were eating pizza in a dorm room, and Johnny's friends were roaming around campus looking for girls to talk to.

Our life together began in a house trailer between the meatpacking plant and a graveyard in Searcy, Arkansas, while we attended Harding University. The thinking that there was no mountain we couldn't climb probably lasted about two weeks until my new husband informed me he wanted to join his friends for a trip to Mardi Gras in New Orleans. "What? Mardi Gras? New Orleans! Single guy friends!" Needless to say, it took a few "discussions" before this young wife was okay with allowing her husband to hit the streets of New Orleans with four friends.

And speaking of New Orleans, no matter how delicious a beignet is (so good!), someone has to put in the hard work to make it go from a dream to a reality. Making a marriage work is challenging even for the most in-love and committed couples. When we announced our upcoming marriage, of course we were met with a few naysayers. "Too young," many declared. But I've never been opposed to young marriages. It seems to be more of a trend today to wait until at least the midtwenties, but that wasn't always the case. All three of our children married young, and two of the marriages ended in divorce. But I'm still not opposed to young marriages.

Here are some of my reasons: Young marriages don't carry the baggage that can come with marrying later in life. Young marriages create a grow-together attitude that gives history to a relationship. Young marriages mean the couple have many firsts together, giving them a bond that marrying older doesn't allow. Young marriages teach spouses to depend on each other as confidants and friends.

Now to the matter of two of our children's marriages ending in divorce. I've spoken a little about this in earlier chapters, and I am committed to not telling any of the details. Those are their stories to share, but I will tell you that the breaking up of their marriages will forever be two of the saddest events in my life.

Divorce is not fun for anyone. I remember telling our daughter Ashley, after we had a deep discussion about how to go forward in life after her divorce, that this was uncharted territory for all of us. While we had faced this trial with our son's marriage ending a year prior to Ashley's, each situation is different and brings its own challenges. No one enters marriage with the goal of divorce, so there's no way to prepare for it. It would be silly to. Everything we did as a family became either new or different. Holidays, graduations, pictures in the hallway and in albums, the grandkids' ball games, and birthday parties—all the family events and customs that brought such joy now carried a weight with them. Have I changed my mind about young marriages because these two didn't make it? No. I firmly believe that the success of any marriage, whether the bride and groom are eighteen or eighty, depends on many things. Age at the time of marriage is just one factor.

I believe people make mistakes and life gets tough and relationships fall apart. I don't believe in the "everything happens for a reason" theology. I believe God has a plan for our lives and that plan includes loving and serving Him and loving others. I believe God's love isn't about Him being happy with us; it's about Him giving us strategies to use to help *us* be happy with *ourselves*. The Bible is filled with advice and proverbs and wisdom that, when applied, can and do help us lead lives that have the scales tipping toward the happy side. Another saying people often quote is "God doesn't care if we're happy; He cares if we're holy." I get it and I agree on most levels. But I believe God does desire that His people are happy too. That's why He gives us rules for living. He knows that if we follow those rules, we will be happier.

As a parent, I want my children to be happy in the sense that I want them to have a spirit of happiness and well-being. I think God feels that way toward us too. Do I believe not being happy is just cause for divorce? No. Not being happy is just cause for working on a marriage and looking to God for help and strength and a changed heart.

Do I believe not being happy is a reason to treat others badly? Never. Not being happy is a reason to "fake it until you make it" at times, but it's important to find out what is the cause of the unhappy demeanor. I do believe being happy with one's life situations makes for a happier and more satisfying marriage. Maybe you're in a job you don't enjoy, or you have neighbors who annoy you, or your children seem to always need something from you. Maybe there are issues you need to address to make your life more pleasant.

When our children were small, there were days and even years when we thought we would never be alone as a couple again. Our relationship was buried under work and kids and commitments and household chores. Then one day the driveway wasn't lined with bicycles, the trampoline was carted off, the swing set rusted, and our house was quiet. The day was finally here. The kids had grown up, and there we were—a couple—just as we were in 1971. Only not exactly. Now it was 1996.

Twenty-five years of raising kids, working on our careers, and building our place in our community meant we were indeed a couple but not the same couple who held hands and crooned the lyrics of this song together. The years when we were raising our family seemed like a whirlwind, a tornado, an earthquake of activities. I'm thankful for cameras (and my poor hubby, who lugged around the huge movie camera!) that captured glimpses of our lives from 1971 to 1996, when our youngest graduated from high school. If not for pictures and videos, the details of those years would have forever disappeared like that disappearing ink pen we loved when we were ten.

I'll never forget my nephew who lived next door coming over to check on us after we returned from leaving our youngest, Ashley, at college. Our sweet nephew Jake, who is a few years younger than Ashley, decided to check on the lonely old couple next door. He really was the sweetest kid. We were just fine, we told him, but we weren't totally fine. We were now a couple learning to live again without kids in the house. And that brought both joy at our newfound freedom and a certain amount of nervousness about our new relationship. I'm happy to say it took only about a week before we realized that we could do life as a couple again and that we really did like each other still. We were grateful for the many marriage seminars we had attended that taught us to keep the fire of our marriage alive with date nights and kind words. For the most part, we had prepared our marriage for this next phase. But our child-free life wasn't totally child-free. We already had a bundle of joy to keep this grandma happy.

John Luke was a year old and Sadie was on the way when our Ashley went off to college, leaving an empty nest. Within five years, we had five grandkids, and in five more years, our grands totaled eleven. Our driveway was once again lined with bicycles, a new trampoline (this time with a safety net) was set up, and the swing set was repainted and repaired. For us, our reintroduced "couple" time was short lived. I found myself, like many new grandmas, consumed with grandma duties. And I loved every minute of it—2-papa, not so much! He had just begun to enjoy walking around the house in his underwear again and having a little more alone time with me.

Many grandparents enjoy living close to their grandchildren and offer daily childcare assistance or just pitch in whenever help is needed. Even if grandparents are still employed, many willingly take on the extra responsibility of helping with the grands. Amid the juggling of all the activities, couples can begin to feel as they did back when their home was filled with their own children. They can drift apart, and one partner can start to feel neglected. In our case, that would be 2-papa, bless his heart. I happen to be married to one of the greats. He is patient, loving, and kind, and more than anything, he desires that I be happy. He knows that my happy place is anywhere the kids are. But I cannot rest on that. I can't depend on 2-papa's good heart and sweet attitude to keep our marriage on track.

How do we grandmas balance our newfound hobby (our grand-kids) and each still keep the man of our dreams happy? And it's more than keeping each other happy. It's about showing our grandkids that our relationship is important and worth working on. I have what I call my ABCs for showing our grandkids that their grandparents are a team and still in love.

Accept Who the Other Is

You would think after all these years, accepting each other's differences would be a given, but it's not. Many older couples seem to do one of three things in dealing with each other's differences:

1. They enjoy complaining about them.

2. They appear to tolerate them.

3. They joyfully celebrate them.

In our marriage, I'm sure we have done all three at different times. But now that we have little ears and eyes hearing and watching us, it's important that we don't do number one or two but lean toward number three. When we started dating, my future husband was the coolest cat in West Monroe, Louisiana. He drove a yellow Cougar Eliminator with a spoiler on the back and black racing stripes down the sides. His hair was long with blond sun-kissed tips. He wore a suede jacket with fringe over his cool T-shirt and bell-bottom jeans. When he came to pick me up at school, all the girls thought I was the luckiest girl in the school, and the guys were insanely jealous.

Well, girls and guys, now my sweet husband is a walking fashion dilemma. His sun-kissed hair is now tipped with gray, and his dreamy green eyes are hidden behind glasses. He wears only Hawaiian-style (that don't tuck in) shirts and comfy shoes with black socks. His idea of cool is now connected only to the thermostat on the air conditioner. I have had to come to terms with the realization that Johnny C, or Johnny Cool, has left the building. At least in terms of outward appearances. On the inside, he's still that cool cat who drove that fancy car.

I've come to realize that we won't look eighteen forever. In fact, I'm pretty sure that's why we lose our vision as we get older. God gifted us with bad vision to soften the wrinkles.

Another great gift of getting older is gaining wisdom. We learn that life isn't about a cool jacket and bell-bottom jeans. As I said earlier, in 2000 Johnny was diagnosed with colon cancer. Because he has a colostomy, Hawaiian-style shirts are the only shirts that work for him. Even though that wasn't him forty-seven years ago, it is him now. Everyone knows him as the guy who wears Hawaiian shirts. Most do not know why; they just think it is his preference. And now it is. Like all things in and out of fashion, apparently Hawaiian shirts are "in" because our grandson Maddox asked to borrow one recently.

From the day Johnny's life changed because of the cancer diagnosis, it was important for both of us to accept his new normal. In every marriage, finding a new normal happens over and over again. It could be because of illness or job choices or kid situations or any number of things, but it's in these new normal times that we are challenged to either solidify our marriage or just tolerate it or leave it. Johnny and I have chosen to embrace whatever comes our way. On those days when I wish I could find another shirt for Johnny to wear, I count my blessings that he's still with us—Hawaiian shirt and all!

Back Each Other Up

Remember how important it was as parents to support each other when you disciplined your kids? Well, being a grandparent requires the same skill set. Your grandchildren need to see that you support each other when it comes to disciplining them or deciding what couch to buy or— this will step on toes—which direction to go when driving to the movie. Johnny and I are notoriously bad travelers together, even though we do it a lot! Our grandkids often travel with us and witness the craziness that ensues when I try to tell 2-papa how to drive or when he tells me where to park. For the most part, all this is done in fun (notice I said

"For the most part"), and the grandkids laugh at our bantering back and forth. But it did occur to me a few years ago that our grands might not enjoy our bantering. We made a decision to be more mindful about our behavior when we travel together. I would say we're a little better now (or at least we think we are). Truth be told, it's easy for couples who have been together for a time to annoy each other while driving or cooking or cleaning or doing anything they do together. Right? And teasing each other can add to the fun of the family dynamics as long as both parties are okay with it. But on important matters, it's always in the best interests of the grandkids to see their grandparents supporting each other.

Every year on Christmas Eve, our extended family (this includes about seventy-five people) has a talent show. We don't exchange gifts; we give the gift of our talent, or lack thereof, to one another. It's a fun night with many laughs and cheers.

One Christmas, 2-papa and I decided (okay, I decided) to lip-synch the song "Love Is an Open Door" from the Disney movie *Frozen*. I was determined that we would practice on the way back from a road trip to see our grands who live in Huntsville, Alabama. I was pumped! We had seven hours to get this song down! But Johnny, who doesn't take these important events as seriously as I do, was not learning the words as quickly as I wanted him to. He kept saying he knew the words, and I kept repeating, "No, you don't!"

I decided to set up the camera on the dashboard and film us. My purpose was to show him how badly he was doing and that he truly didn't know the words. What resulted was a video that actually be-came our talent for Christmas Eve. When we played it back, we realized it would be much better to surprise the kids with this video than for us to do it live. And it was! We had never done anything like that, so you can imagine the looks of disbelief and shock on our grandkids' faces (remember, it's always good to keep the kids guessing). We prefaced the viewing by telling our grandkids we love being with them but they have no idea what we do when they aren't around, so we thought we would show them. Then we played the video. It's still on YouTube if you want to look. (Just put in my name and "*Frozen* song" and it will come up.) The point of this story is just to tell you to look for ways for your grands to see you working together, having fun, and loving each other.

On another note, I have been the director at a summer camp for over thirty years. That means for more than thirty summers, I have spent many nights out at the camp without 2-papa. Even though he loves the camp and supports it 100 percent, he's not interested in spending the night out there anymore. (There was a time when he loved it, but this is not that time.) Still, he allows me to. I love that he accepts my love of camping and allows me to do what I love to do. He comes out for dinner occasionally, but for the most part, he lets me do my thing.

What do I do for him? Well, this is a weird one, but I don't love to eat like 2-papa does. I try to be supportive of his love for food by going to different restaurants with him. I would be happy with a bowl of cereal for supper, but that won't do for 2-papa. Consequently, we are (at least, he is) always on the search for the next best meal.

Giving each other the freedom to be who we are is still one of the greatest gifts we can give each other in marriage. Growing old together means letting you be you and me be me—together. That reminds me of another song, one by the Turtles, "So Happy Together." Remember these lyrics? "I can't see me lovin' nobody but you for all my life."[3] You can't sustain the kind of love that makes you happy together without accepting each other and each other's interests.

Communicate

Communication is still the key to a good relationship. We were told this at the first marriage retreat we signed up to attend. We had probably been married five years and already had three little ones at home. That weekend, a good marriage retreat would have been two days of sleep for me and a delicious meal for Johnny. (Okay, that would have been his second choice. We won't go into his first choice.) Instead of being allowed to sleep late, we were up bright and early for the first class. After a lecture, we were told to go back to our rooms and describe various feelings using only colors. I seriously thought I was going to pull my hair out. Johnny tends to be very literal, and he's a rule follower. The assignment was basically a disaster. It was an exercise in patience for me as he struggled to describe how he felt in different scenarios using the color wheel. While the whole weekend wasn't as productive as it should have been, we have laughed about the "color conference" for years.

We did pump up our communication skills that weekend and at other marriage conferences throughout our marriage. Like many other things in our marriage, we've learned that Johnny and I communicate in opposite ways. One example of this is the type of cards we like to give for birthdays and anniversaries. He loves to give me cards with lots of writing on them, *and* he underlines the important lines, *and* he loves to read every word out loud to me. I like cards with no more than ten words on them, and those words are usually funny. As a result, I've learned to give him cards he likes to receive (with lots of underlined words) and to listen attentively while he reads his cards to me.

A good marriage must include looking for the ways the other person communicates and using that approach. This is part of the "Platinum Rule," as Johnny calls it. I'm sure he read it somewhere, but it's a favorite of his. We all know the Golden Rule: "Do unto others as you would have them do unto you." The problem with this rule is it implies that other people want to be treated as you would like to be treated, which is rarely the case because we're all different. The Platinum Rule says, "Treat others the way *they* want to be treated." This makes more sense, doesn't it? If I am looking for the ways Johnny wants to be treated instead of how I want to be treated, I will focus on him, not on myself.

For instance, in communication, Johnny processes information on the outside, and I process information on the inside. I know that sounds crazy, but here's the simple explanation: Johnny says everything he thinks, and I keep what I'm thinking to myself. Again, we're total opposites. I have learned to listen to his talking and know that some of the words coming out are just him working through a problem. He's had to adjust to my being quiet until I have the response firmly planted in my head. The way people communicate is partly due to their personality and partly driven by past experiences. Rarely is it our desire to upset or cause trouble with our spouse. But this is not always an easy bridge to cross. If we will always remember to go back to what we know (he loves me and wants the best for me) instead of what we feel (he must not love me because he keeps doing that thing that makes me crazy), then we will stay on top of communication problems.

Date

Date nights equal a fun marriage. It's easy for a long-term relationship to get stagnant. *I mean, seriously! We've been together for forty-seven years!* Forty-seven years means there is a lot of history behind us. One of the most interesting things to me about relationships is how the very things that attracted a person to her spouse could very well be the things that make her completely crazy later in the relationship. When we were first married, I loved how Johnny would call a waitress over by raising his hand in the air. I thought he was cool and commanding. Now when he does the same gesture, I think he's bossy and demanding. For his part, he's not thinking anything; there's no motive attached to his technique. That's just how he gets the waitress's attention. When we were young, I loved that he kept a list in his pocket to remind him of jobs to do. (Remember, I'm a list maker too.) But he's not just a list maker. He's a rule follower, even about his own rules. He will stick with that list no matter what else is going on. If he hasn't crossed off number seven on the list, he will keep at it until it's gone.

The little things that annoy each person in a relationship add up to big things, resulting in couples pulling away from each other. This is why date nights are still important. No matter what age you are, being able to enjoy each other's company keeps the spark lit and the relationship fun. It does other things, too, such as strengthening your commitment to the relationship, reminding you why you chose each other in the first place, relieving stress from the pressures of life, and letting others know you value your marriage and want to spend time with each other. Many times the grands have called us to see whether we could take them somewhere or do something with them, and I've explained that I have a date with 2-papa that night and can't make it. I know that underneath their disappointment, their brains are registering what a loving couple does to keep a relationship healthy.

Evaluate

It's always valuable to stop and take stock of where your marriage is. Sadly, after thirty or forty years, many couples decide it is what it is and it can't be changed. This isn't true. We have a ministry at our church called Re/engage, which is designed to help couples of all ages and in all stages develop a more loving relationship. I've seen couples who were on the brink of divorce and couples who were content to live in a place of "good enough" become couples who burst with love and passion again. Don't settle for good enough. If you need guidance to strengthen your marriage, look for it through a program like Re/engage. You could probably google ways to strengthen your marriage and find plenty of tips online as well. Or pick up a good book.

There are many ways to evaluate your marriage and take it to the next level, whatever that is for you and your spouse. But don't settle. Even in your more mature years, it's important to find a way to enjoy each other's company. Think back to what you used to do. Was it a card game? Or a walk by the river? Or a tennis match? Go back to the beginning and start doing those things again.

Forgive

The secret to any relationship is the ability to forgive. Life includes many little mistakes. I'm not talking about the big ones here; I'm talking about the daily ones that can build up to be the big ones. Little mistakes help us learn and take us to the next level of understanding in whatever it is we're working on.

Do you remember when you were learning to ride a bicycle? It was the mistakes you made as you tried to pedal successfully that led you to work harder and finally get it right, sailing smoothly and confidently down the street. The mistakes we make when learning to ride a bike are child's play compared with the mistakes we make daily in our marriages. Some mistakes are truly accidental, because we might hurt our spouse's feelings unintentionally. Others are quite intentional, right? We often find ourselves trying to out-shout, out-argue, out-cut down, or out-hurt the one who has offended us. We soon realize that retaliation does nothing to bring us closer to each other or to God.

The Bible and research both back up the fact that when forgiveness is given, the one doing the forgiving gains a boatload of blessings. A reduction in depression, increased hopefulness, and decreased anger are just some of the reported benefits of simply forgiving the one who has offended you.[4]

The bottom line is clearly understanding that we all make mistakes and are all in need of forgiveness. It's the principle that says three fingers are pointing back at you when you are pointing at another. As Jesus forgave us, we must forgive others. Always remember that the choice to forgive will affect generations to come.

I firmly believe if our grandkids benefit from any one thing we do as grandparents, it would be showing them what a faithful, loving, committed relationship looks like. We are the senior backbone of society. I hope you wholeheartedly accept that responsibility. The older couples of any society are the ones setting the pace, leading the race, and laying the foundation for faith-filled families and a better world. A strong patriarch and matriarch of a family give the family a sense of

Rockstar GRANDPARENTING

Growing old together means letting you be you and me be me—together.

purpose and direction. From these determined leaders, children and grandchildren form opinions about themselves and what their place in the world is. I'll talk more about our role as leaders in our family in chapter 10. Just know you and your spouse are a much-needed support for the younger generation.

When Johnny and I were younger, we disliked the word *comfortable,* and we used to look sadly at older couples in restaurants who were not talking to each other. What we saw were couples who had settled for a comfortable life—a boring life. We didn't want to be a boring couple. We didn't want to be a couple who didn't have any words left and perhaps tolerated each other's quirks and craziness.

Now that we are older, we know that being quiet doesn't mean there is no joy in the relationship. It might mean we've said enough words today so we're enjoying silence together. It might mean we're close enough that words don't have to be used to communicate. It might mean we're happy with each other even if we don't want to talk. It might mean we're hungry and just want to eat. Mostly, I've learned, silence might mean that our actions speak louder than words. And those silent couples are ones who have stayed together through good times and bad.

———

The believing wife brings holiness to her marriage, and the believing husband brings holiness to his marriage. Otherwise, your children would not be holy, but now they are holy.

—1 CORINTHIANS 7:14

Leader of the Pack

*Y*ou might be wondering whether this song performed by the group with the bad-girl image, the Shangri-Las, is suitable for our playlist of grandparenting tunes. Well, the title is on target, but the lyrics . . . well, they are too, and here's why.

As grandparents, we are the leaders of our pack. Whether you look at your family tree and see only a couple of brackets leading to five or six names or a hundred, you are the leaders of the group of people who are placed under your name and that of your spouse.

This song tells the story of Betty, who falls in love with Jimmy, the leader of a motorcycle pack. His bad-boy image doesn't sit well with Betty's parents, and they tell her she has to break up with him. (Wow! Parents could do that in 1964!) The tragic story ends with Jimmy driving away on his motorcycle on a rainy night and Betty screaming at him to slow down. The leader of the pack was gone. Betty was left to mourn her lost love and wonder what could have been.[1]

As grandparents, our fate probably won't include a motorcycle and a rainy night, but there will come a time when our lives will be over, and the things we have left behind will tell the stories of the lives we lived. I don't want to get too psychological, because it's not my field, but I do want to bring up an interesting study done by Erik Erikson (1902–1994). Erikson was best known for his work in psychosocial behavior. In other words, his studies looked at how our thinking and personality determine or interact with our social life. Many doctors in the psychiatric community at the time Erikson was working had presented theories that focused on early childhood events and influences, but Erikson looked at how social influences contribute to personality throughout the entire life span. This is where his studies relate to us and the importance of leading our families.

Erikson stated that we live in stages. Johnny and I know this to be true because we have watched our children go through childhood. We often talked about each stage and the importance of our children hitting the markers necessary to move from one stage to the next. When you think about it, it makes sense that those stages don't stop just because we reach adulthood.

For this discussion, we'll start with stage 7 in Erikson's study. Stage 7 is described as middle adulthood when many of us become grandparents. He calls that stage "Generativity vs. Stagnation." We're from Louisiana, which means we know a thing or two about stagnation, as in stagnant water. It gets green and slimy and is a breeding ground for mosquitoes and snakes. By definition, *stagnant* means "having stopped growing and developing." *Generativity* is a term coined by Erikson that simply means "a concern for establishing and guiding the next generation."

During adulthood, according to Erikson's study, a natural development would be for one to focus on one's career and family. Those who are successful during this phase will develop a sense of fulfillment, feeling as if their work as the leader of their family has contributed to society as a whole. Those who fail at this stage will feel unproductive and uninvolved in what is going on in the world, leading to feelings of poor self-worth. This is confirmation that we need to take on this responsibility as leaders of our pack, not just for the future generations but also for ourselves to live with meaning and focus. It's in everyone's best interests that we get to a place where we enjoy watching our children and grandchildren take their role as adults in society. Our fulfillment will come from watching them use the tools we've given them to build their families and start their careers.

The final stage Erikson talked about is "Integrity vs. Despair." This stage is a few years down the road for most of us, but as the old saying goes, "If you don't know where you're going, you'll end up someplace else." It's important to be mindful now so that our future will be secure. In this final stage of development, we will reflect on our lives to determine whether we are happy with the choices we made or wish we could have done better. Obviously, those who feel proud of their accomplishments will finish out their days with a sense of integrity, a state of feeling whole and being honest about their lives. Those who are not happy and feel as if they didn't do what needed to be done will be left with feelings of despair.[2]

While my husband and I are in the stage of life that offers us fewer days, we are not content to be done yet. We still have a family to lead and children to influence for good. Our job is to leave a legacy for our children and grandchildren that will cause them to continue to fight for what is right and good. A legacy is simply what people want to pass down to their offspring.

The Bible often speaks about heritage and legacy living. Psalm 78:4 says,

We will not hide these truths from our children;
   we will tell the next generation
about the glorious deeds of the LORD,
   about his power and his mighty wonders.

And the apostle John wrote,

I could have no greater joy than to hear that my children are
following the truth. (3 John 4)

From these verses—and there are many more—we see the importance of leaving the things we value to our children and grandchildren.
Business ideas, valued principles, lifestyle choices, family recipes, favorite traditions, and, if there is any left, money are all examples of the
kinds of things people value and want to leave with their family when
they are gone. Sadly, many families fight over the money left to them
after the death of a loved one, when it's the intangible things that really
hold the most importance.

In our family, even though three of the great-grandparents have
gone on to heaven, we still verbalize the heritage they left with our
grandchildren. Some of my grandchildren were old enough to remember them before they died, but most were not. We keep their memories
alive by speaking about them and sharing the things they did while on
this earth. We don't do this to hold what they did over anyone's head or
to brag. We do this with love and respect for the things they accomplished in life.

Our grandkids know that Papaw Howard is the reason they can go to Camp Ch-Yo-Ca every summer and learn about God. The Christian school they attend is there because of men and women like their great-grandparents. Their pictures hang in the hall of the school, reminding others of sacrifices that were made for the school to be here today.

The grandchildren know that Papaw Shack loved basketball, not just for the game itself but for the lessons learned while playing. His picture hangs in the basketball gym of the Christian school because of his love and support of the teams that played there. Both of these fine men are part of my grandchildren's legacy, and I'm grateful my grandchildren can know some of their history.

I realize not all families have a history that can be honored and praised and held up as a standard for living. If that's the case for you, you get to be the game changer, the difference maker. The buck stops with you. You are now the leader of the pack. From this generation on, you can change the fruit growing on your family tree.

My father's dad was an alcoholic who left his family. My daddy said, "No more!" and chose to lead his family down a different path, one of faith and love. It wasn't because he saw it modeled; it was because he made a decision to make better choices.

How do we do it? What are some things we do to leave a legacy of the things our family values?

Attend Church Together

Church attendance is declining even though the Bible makes it clear that belonging to a church is good for everyone involved. Not just because it is an act of obedience and love to God, but also because belonging to a church family offers support and help to those who are bound together and determined to keep the schemes of the devil away from them. Church is about being with others who inspire, motivate, and encourage you to be a better person. Who wouldn't want those people to also be the people you are related to by blood? Much of our family attends the same church. We love seeing one another on Sunday mornings. We love the fact that on any given Sunday, our grandkids might have an uncle leading the singing, a grandparent speaking, an aunt teaching a Bible class, or a cousin saying a prayer or playing piano on the worship team. We believe there is nothing better for children than seeing their family live out their faith by worshipping together.

You may not live in the same town as your family, or you may choose a different fellowship to worship with. That's okay. When we visit our grands who live in another town, we love worshipping with them and seeing what their fellowship is doing in their community. We are careful to be positive and supportive about the body of people they have chosen to fellowship with. You don't have to go to the same church to share your church journey. On occasion, I will call my grands who live out of town just to ask them about church that morning. This lets them know I value what they are doing and it's important to me to stay connected with them concerning their church fellowship time.

Keep Traditions Alive

Family traditions are an important piece of the puzzle because they tell family members they are a part of something bigger than themselves. It builds a sense of security in children as they learn to depend on certain things happening year after year. These traditions are designed to communicate that our family loves one another enough to do whatever the tradition is every year. The generation before mine, which lived through World War II, didn't have time for traditions like we see today. I don't know that my parents gave any thought to starting traditions. That wasn't modeled for them—survival was modeled for them—but they lived in such a way that their children wanted to carry on the things they did.

Here are two important things to remember about traditions: (1) do not let them become family burdens, and (2) realize that traditions can, and often do, change. For many years, our family enjoyed the tradition of spending Christmas Eve at my parents' home. As my siblings and I got older and our kids got bigger, it became clear that the tradition should be moved to my house. I'm blessed that I saw my mom and dad model the behavior I need to have when it becomes time to move the celebration from my house to the house of someone in the next generation. I'm sure my mom felt a little displaced the first year the Christmas celebration was not in her home, but she didn't show it. She pitched in and did whatever was needed to ensure the night was a success, and she continued to be the leader of the family that she still is to this day. In fact, soon she added a new tradition—the annual Christmas brunch. Now this brunch is how we start the holiday season. It's usually held the Saturday before Christmas, but that's not written in stone either. Mom is flexible enough to have the brunch at the most convenient time for the majority of the family. She treats us to the likes of cinnamon rolls, bananas Foster, and coffee punch.

When Johnny's parents were alive, Papaw Howard had what was

called the Howard Family Christmas Night. Oh, how he loved Christmas! There were singing and skits and stockings and good food. With the deaths of Mamaw and Papaw Howard, that tradition died. But other traditions have taken its place, and it's because of what Papaw and Mamaw Howard did that new traditions have cropped up.

Our family has tried to live by the motto of flexibility (again, a legacy handed down from our parents) when it comes to things like birthday celebrations and holiday events. We treat these events as important, but there are more important things going on in the world. Very rarely do family members get to have a birthday party on the day of their birthday. We try to get together once a month for family birthday time. We might be celebrating six or seven people that day, but we love our tradition of honoring one another.

We have a GroupMe app on our phones that allows us to keep up with important family events and announcements. And we strive not to make people feel guilty if they cannot attend. This is very important. There's a fine line between teaching that supporting family is important and putting someone on a guilt trip. (If I've crossed that line a few times, I'm sorry. It wasn't done intentionally, but I might be guilty!)

Attend Important Events

This is a continuation of the last idea of building a legacy of family values, but the events I'm talking about here are things like graduations, dance recitals, ball games, weddings, births, baptisms, and anything the person who is being honored or who is performing feels it's important to be at. Okay, this can make you crazy. Right up front, let me say that attending every event your kids and grandkids have going on is impossible. Trust me—I have tried. Just do the math for your family. Here's mine: I have three children who are all married and have blessed me with fourteen grandchildren—now two of the grandkids are married. My family of five is now a family of twenty-four. Here are my mom's numbers: Mom's family started out as a family of eight (I have five siblings). Four of my siblings are married and produced twelve grandkids. Nine of them are married. She has twenty-eight great-grandkids. Two of them are married. Her grand total of important people to enjoy is sixty-one! That's why it's impossible to go to every event of every member in your family.

Here's how it works in our family. We all do what we can to show love and support to everyone in the family, and we don't take any of it for granted. Jealousy has no place at the table of a family who is trying to love and serve God and one another. One thing we have access to now in our tech-savvy world and take advantage of is a family group-messaging app on our phones. It allows us to stay updated on the various activities we have going on. We encourage, congratulate, and sympathize with family members as new messages pop up each day.

As grandparents, we just have to do what we can and not worry about the rest. I've heard some grandparents claim they can't get to all events so they choose not to go to any events. I'm sorry, but that doesn't make sense to me. Obviously, those grandparents don't want to go to any events. That's okay. We all have to make choices in life. I just happen to believe family shows up for family, if possible. This is how I was raised. When I was growing up, my parents encouraged us to attend the ball games my brothers were playing in. Not all, but most. My poor brothers were dragged to my synchronized swimming events (sorry, bros). But in doing that, we learned that family supports family.

Johnny and I do our best to be at the events our grands are involved in. When Sadie was chosen to be on *Dancing with the Stars,* it was important to our family that a family member be there with her. Korie was filming *Duck Dynasty* at the time, which meant she couldn't go. I was the one to do it. During those three months, I missed events my other grandkids had, but our family understood the importance of Sadie's new assignment. I stayed in touch with the other grandkids through FaceTime (I've watched many volleyball games on my phone), texts, and phone calls, telling them how proud I was of them. Not being able to attend an event should never be confused with not supporting or loving a grandchild. If that is the message grandchildren are getting, someone is dropping the ball.

Children, whether they are grandkids or your own kids, should be taught to be thankful for anyone choosing to come support them. I'm proud to say my grands always thank me for attending their events. They've been taught well. (Thank you to my children, who reinforce the importance of good manners! Side note: Sadie was listed number five in a 2017 list of celebrities who have good manners.[3] Love it!)

In 2009, 2-papa and I went to England to study at Oxford University for a semester. We were asked to attend by one of our friends, who was on staff that semester. It was a tough call for me because I truly don't like to be away from my family. But good sense (and 2-papa's pleading) finally won out, and off we went for our England adventure. Our Christian school puts on an elaborate Grandparents Day production (seriously, I'm talking Broadway level—okay, maybe not, but awesome) the week before Thanksgiving. That year was to be our granddaughter Bella's first time to perform. Of course, we were in England and couldn't possibly be there. We did the next best thing (or so we thought) and watched it on Skype. Apparently that wasn't good enough, because Bella, who is now sixteen, seems to have marked time by the year we missed her Grandparents Day performance. She brings it up nearly every year! We know our missing this event didn't have any huge bearing on her entire life journey, but she felt the impact of our absence. I don't take that lightly. Even little things like this can become part of your family history that defines and connects you and your grandchildren. We laugh at Bella holding this over our grandparenting heads (and she does!), but inside, I do feel a little guilty and very loved that she missed us not being there.

State Family Values (Out Loud)

There are many things your family values that will be handed down by observation, and this is important. I'm a huge supporter of modeling right behavior. But children are not always going to learn what they need to learn simply by watching. They also need to be told. Words are a powerful tool that can be used for both good and bad.

Recently we met a man whose dad had berated him, telling him he was worthless and wouldn't amount to anything. He spent a lifetime trying to measure up and show his dad that he was valuable. His dad committed suicide, leaving this man without hope of showing him that he did amount to something. He longed for words of affirmation from his dad. Just before his mom died, he confronted her, asking whether he really was as bad as his dad told him he was. She said, "No, you were a normal boy. Your dad was a jerk."

Oh, how he wished she had said those words to him fifty years earlier. They could have prevented years of anxiety, insecurity, self-hatred, doubt, and a list of other horrible emotions this man struggled with because of the words his dad spoke over him. Our words have power.

Over the years, I have spoken to countless men and women who credit their grandparents with changing the course of their lives—grandparents who spoke integrity and encouragement and love into their grandkids. It's important that you speak family values into your grandchildren. It's not bragging but truth to tell your grandchildren things such as

- In our family, we always tell the truth.
- In our family, we seek out those who need help, and we help them.
- In our family, we stand beside one another when we are hurting.
- In our family, we don't cover up mistakes but support the one who made them and help her overcome them.

A few years ago the Robertson family had a musical written about them (little-known fact). One of their favorite songs was titled "When You're a Robertson." The lyrics told of the things the Robertson family stands for and stated that being a Robertson is an important position to hold. Every family should have the feeling that a song could be written about what it means to be in their family. We hope we have lived in such a way that our grandchildren know what we stand for and believe that being a Howard descendant is a good thing.

Tell your grandchildren the important stories about your family.

Don't be intimidated when they have a cell phone or video game in their hands (that's nearly always). Tell them you have important facts and stories to tell them about their family. Then share a story that lets them know what it means to be a _____ (fill in your last name). Anytime you get a chance, reinforce your family values using specific examples, as I did in the list above. Remember this: children rarely pay attention the first time, so repetition is important.

Our family also believes in the importance of a family mission statement. I encourage you to develop one for your family. It makes for a fun night of discussion if you can get everyone together and involved in writing it. If you don't live close enough for that, do it by group text or wait until the next time you are all together. Any thriving business operates according to its mission statement. Our families are more important than any business. Doesn't it make sense to treat them with the same intensity and dedication?

Our family mission is to be together in heaven for all eternity and to take many others with us. We will do this by letting people see Jesus in us every day. We will show the world we care by the way we share. We will love unconditionally and work at lending support to one another so every family member will feel valued and loved and will grow spiritually. We will pray regularly that the Spirit of Jesus will be seen in each one of us and that we will pass on our legacy of principles for living to our children and grandchildren (see appendix 2).

Vacation Together

I will leave to sociologists whether the following statement is true and just scream out what all of us moms and grandmas feel: "We are busier than anyone has ever been in the history of the world!" I don't know whether statistics back this up, but it certainly seems as if it's true. I remember a time when sports had distinct seasons. Now coaches call every sport a year-round sport. I have one grandson who juggles basketball, soccer, and baseball year-round. It's enough to make you crazy! Not to mention the Christmas season that now starts in October. Each holiday used to stand on its own, but now Halloween, Thanksgiving, and Christmas are all on the shelves at the same time. When I'm picking up a pumpkin, I feel as though I'm behind on my Christmas shopping.

Then there's the pressure that social media puts on us. In a very recent past, no one except your immediate family knew if you baked a cake or decorated your house or went on a diet. Now, because we share that information with a few thousand of our friends, we feel pressured to do it more often or do it better.

Maybe it's not that we're busier but that we have many more options of things to do. People today stay in a constant state of choice burnout. No matter what the reason, the reality is we are all busy. I've heard that "Busy" is the new "Good" for a response to the question "How are you?"

First of all, let's get this clear: busy isn't necessarily bad. From the beginning, God created us to work. While in the perfect garden, where everything needed was supplied, God told Adam and Eve to tend to the garden. We're told in the book of Proverbs that lazy hands produce poverty (see Proverbs 10:4). Other scriptures support the fact that God detests idle behavior, not busy behavior. Didn't our grandmothers tell us that idle hands are the devil's workshop? I know I heard that somewhere. But aren't we too busy? Don't we all need to slow down? Well, that depends on what you're spending your time doing. Only you can answer that question.

We do know that God invites us to rest. Ahhhh . . . that sounds good, doesn't it? The word *rest* just sounds . . . restful. We should understand that being idle is not the same thing as resting. Resting implies taking a break from the work you are doing. Being idle means you have nothing substantial going on. *Idle* is another word for "lazy." If you put your cursor over the word *lazy, idle* comes up as a synonym. I am a firm believer—and I saw it modeled in my parents and in-laws—that God didn't put an age limit on being an active participant in the Lord's army. My eighty-seven-year-old mom (I know I keep throwing her in here, but she's remarkable) is still marching in the Lord's army, hosting a house church, mentoring younger women, and cooking for those in need. Our parents who are now in God's army in heaven did the same. But they also understood the important of rest.

Our family has always enjoyed vacationing together. From beach vacations to ski trips to amusement park outings, vacationing together has been our way of reconnecting after months of busyness. God values our rest time. It's a time to regroup and get ready to go again at full speed. Much can be accomplished in these periods of rest.

When our children were growing up, we started a list we call *Our Legacy of Principles for Living.* On every vacation, we took the time to add to our legacy list. Each person thought of something we wanted to live out in our family and ultimately leave to the world. I've included the list in the back of this book if you want to see what ours looks like. You might want to start this with your family. It will surprise you how deeply your little people can think. For us, it reinforced our family values and helped our children take ownership of the values for themselves. We did this during our vacations because it was a good time to have the kids trapped in a room with us.

Aside from our regular vacations, as our grands got older, we took them, a few at a time, on a special trip. This allowed us quality time with our teenage grands, which is hard to squeeze in any other time. Our last four teenage grandkids joined us in the fall of 2018. Since they are the youngest, they had the longest time to think about the trip. They watched two other sets of cousins go and come back with fun stories. In some ways, being the youngest might have made the trip more special, as they had to wait the longest, or at least it seemed like it to them.

One more thing we've done as our grands have gotten older. Not every year, but on some years, we've done away with Christmas presents in order to take our entire family on a mission trip or some other meaningful experience. A few years ago we partnered with Roma Boots to deliver rain boots to needy children in Guatemala. Our grands will never forget that Christmas. Instead of getting gifts, they gave the gift of themselves to others.

I've already mentioned this, but I warned you it would come up again. In 2017 we went to Israel in place of store-bought Christmas gifts, and I made each child a gift that held special meaning. For instance, our Macy is our fashionista. She's now nineteen years old, but when she was four, I was repairing one of the smocked dresses I had made for one of my daughters and getting it ready for Macy to wear. She asked me what I was doing, and when I told her, she said, "You can give that dress to Sadie. It's not my style." (Not my style! Are you kidding me? Oh well!) I framed one of the smocked dresses along with a picture of her in that dress as her Christmas gift. I hope it will always make her smile as she remembers her sassy little comment and will remind her of her grandmother who smocked dresses for her and her cousins. I did something similar for each of my children and grandchildren. Everyone has declared that that Christmas was the best Christmas ever. Israel and homemade gifts were a hit!

While some vacations or activities are planned to intentionally bring closeness to the family or awareness of the world around us, most of our vacation time is designed for us to laugh, play, grow, create memories, and rest together. There are many ways to use travel time.

Please Sweat the Small Stuff

There will be many, many little things you do as the leaders of your family that will become big things to your grandkids. You often won't even know how they will influence your family until the kids are older and can tell you.

An example of one of our smallest traditions is that when we're traveling and come across the sign that tells us we're in another state, 2-papa always yells "Two states." Now it's become a tradition. All our grands yell "Two states" together when crossing a border.

Another little tradition was started by my mom when we were growing up. When we leave for a trip, we burst out with the chorus from an old song called "Cuanto La Gusta" by Carmen Miranda and the Andrews Sisters, which is featured in the MGM movie *A Date with Judy.* It was released in the '40s—way before our time, right? My mother is credited with keeping the song alive, at least within our family, but we've struggled with getting the lyrics correct. Instead of ending the song with "Cuanto la gusta," we sing, "Juan dela goose, dela goose." I seriously don't know who came up with "Juan dela goose," but we've been singing it for years, and this song has brought many laughs and fun times to our family.

★ ★ ★ ★
Rockstar
GRANDPARENTING

You are now the leader of the pack. From this generation on, you can change the fruit growing on your family tree.

One other little tradition happens every time (seriously, every time) 2-papa comes in the back door. He yells "Ho, ho, ho." Now that our grandkids are older, they love to come in our back door yelling "Ho, ho, ho!" Those three words say "I'm here," "I love you," "This is our family," "You matter," and much more. It's the little things that communicate *huge* messages of love to our kids.

Your family will have its own traditions that distinguish your family from others. As the leaders of your pack, be aware of adding fun things to your time together that will tell your grands, "This is *us*." And remember, the fun things don't have to be big things; the small things matter just as much.

Shine Your Light

We all have to determine for ourselves how to let our lights shine in the world. We're going to cover shining a light for Jesus more in the final chapter of the book, but while we're talking about leading, I want to add that being a light that shines in your community, church, or country is the best way to lead your family. One of the things I love about Facebook is keeping up with friends who walked through the glory days of the '60s and '70s with me. It makes my heart happy to read of their accomplishments and see that everyone eventually grew out of the '60s peace, love, and rock-and-roll mentality and became hard workers, dedicated family men and women, and patriotic citizens. I like to think of our whole world as a high school with its different groups of people—some athletes, some mathematicians, some musicians. God was brilliant to create all of us differently, right? It truly takes everyone to make a world go around, and there are many places for us to shine.

In real life, shining doesn't mean being the president of your class or team captain or first-chair clarinet player. This is where life differs from high school. Shining in real life means making a difference in the lives of those around you. We all are aware that the smallest night-light is valuable when taking a trip to the bathroom in the middle of the night. Your light doesn't have to be the biggest and brightest light to make an impact on your family. You have to shine only enough to affect your corner of the world with love and happiness.

I have a precious memory of Sadie and Macy combing 2-papa's hair into the craziest hairdo while we rode the subway to the US Open on one of our grandkid trips to New York. Sometimes I think 2-papa puts the "grand" in the word *grandparenting,* and I put the "parent" in it. He's always willing to do anything the kids want to do, while I feel more of a responsibility to teach them things. As a tennis player, I eagerly anticipated the day at the US Open. I was excited to teach the kids about the game and the level of work it takes to get to the Open, but the kids will never remember who played that day or who won. They will remember 2-papa letting them fix his hair and everyone on the subway laughing at him. In that moment, 2-papa was a shining example of letting go and having fun with his grandkids.

My husband shines in other ways too, such as leading his publishing company to receive the award for being the best Christian workplace seven years in a row, serving as an elder at our local church, and being on the board of our Christian school, but for our grandkids, he's the one who will let them play with his hair. There's no amount of money or fame that can take the place of making your grandkids feel loved, protected, and supported. They won't care if you own the company or if you won the Super Bowl, but they will remember you chasing them around the living room, growling like a bear, or bringing them cookies before a big game.

Shining as grandparents is the easiest shine we'll ever do. It doesn't require much, but it offers everything.

———

You yourself must be an example to them by doing good works of every kind. Let everything you do reflect the integrity and seriousness of your teaching.

—Titus 2:7

★ ★ ★ ★ ★

11

When I'm Sixty-Four

*I*f you are like me, you can still remember singing the words "When I get older, losing my hair, many years from now . . ."[1] and smiling or laughing at the thought of your true love being bald and possibly forgetting to send you a valentine. Then we woke up to discover we are sixty-four or pretty close or we're seeing sixty-four in the rearview mirror! This song written by Paul McCartney is a simple one—it's the tale of two lovers growing old together and the life they might possibly be living at that age. The lyrics say the woman in the song might be knitting a sweater; the man might be tending a garden. But most of all, the question seems to be, Will they still need each other in their older years?

Aging is a funny animal, isn't it? I just turned sixty-four while writing this book, and I have to admit it doesn't look anything like I thought it would when I sang this song at thirteen or fourteen or sixteen years of age. It's reported that Sir Paul was fifteen when he wrote this song, which tells me he must have been very observant of the older generation. Perhaps he was close to grandparents or aunts and uncles who lived a quiet life that included knitting and gardening and Sunday drives in the country. I don't know. But I do remember, as I said earlier, what my grandparents' lives looked like, and they included all those things. (Do you remember when going for a Sunday drive was actually a family activity? Today we might go to a movie or the zoo. Not back then. We would just drive around. Obviously, we were easy to entertain.)

In any case, I don't think sixty-four is considered old today. I'm sure at a good ten years past sixty-four, Paul McCartney would agree. Even my grandchildren say I'm not old. In fact, they don't even like it when I say I'm old. It's funny how our perception of old has changed over the years. Someone said old age is twenty years older than you are. That might be a good definition. Here's my question: Why do we consider ourselves still young when we're the same age that old people used to be? Does that question make sense? In other words, why are we still young when we're old? Age is age, one would think. But in my humble opinion, there are many things that contribute to us being younger "old" folks.

It's no secret that better medicine and a heathier lifestyle certainly contribute to a longer life. But that can't be the only answer. Don't we look younger too? How are we looking younger? Here's one answer. We think younger. I remember when I was growing up, the only time I would be tempted to wear my grandmothers' clothes would be at Halloween, yet my grandkids constantly raid my closet for jeans, shirts, and shoes. On top of better medicine and a healthier diet, we baby boomers refuse to think of ourselves as old. While there used to be a distinct difference in what an older person should and should not wear or do, those lines are blurred now. Our generation has always subscribed to the motto "If it feels good, do it." I admit, it was used incorrectly many times, but what we were really saying is "Don't put us in a box," whether it was with our clothes, job choices, music, or lifestyle. We have embraced wearing skinny jeans, leggings (with a long top), and longer hair, even if we're over fifty. All these things are part of our outward appearance and are insignificant in the scheme of important things, but they contribute to our younger attitude.

And speaking of attitude, thinking our way into a better way of living has long been proven as an important tool in our psychological toolbox. At the summer camp I direct, we have an exercise that we call an attitude check. It goes like this: When we see the campers dragging or having a bad attitude, we yell, "Attitude check!" The campers have to reply, "I feel great. Oh, I feel so great!" Then they have to grunt loudly and pump their fists. Invariably, their attitudes change and we have happy campers once again. Our attitude about aging can be the difference maker in whether we feel old or young. Whether we *are* old or not doesn't matter; how we *feel* does matter. (This is one of the few times I acknowledge that feelings can outweigh facts.)

There are many factors that go into feeling good at whatever age you are, and I don't want to diminish the fact that serious illnesses can keep us from feeling our best. Johnny and I have both had serious illnesses, as well as major injuries, that have kept us on the sidelines of life for a while, but the trick is to get back to how you were before the illness or accident as closely and as quickly as you can. We now know that when our grandparents retired to rocking chairs, it wasn't good for them. Bodies in movement stay in movement. Right? Better medicine, a healthier diet, a young attitude, and more movement all contribute to a younger you and me.

Let's look at a few more things that will keep us young and feeling good.

Pay Attention to Yourself

As we get older, we do have to pay more attention to ourselves. I say this is why we don't have little kids in our old age. It's enough to take care of ourselves! My mom is funny about this. She says she has reached the point in her life when her calendar is filled with things that help her maintain life, such as doctor's appointments. She's right. In many ways, we do have to turn our attention to ourselves if we want to stay healthy. When I was younger, I loved going to the gym and working out. But I considered it a luxury on my long to-do list. If I had time, I went to the gym. Today it's a necessity. I try to do something physical at least three times a week. I don't always go to a gym. Now I prefer to work out at home with free weights or walk or play tennis or do anything to get moving. It is now essential and on my to-do list, not to be missed.

Hang Out with Young People

I heard some great advice the other day. It said every old person should have a young friend. I love that. Even though I have lots of grandkids, I still value time with other young people besides my own grands. It keeps me young and up to date on what is going on in their world. Johnny and I have hosted a worship time for the teens at our church for nearly forty years. Every Sunday night teens come over and our house is filled with great praise music, laughter, and learning about God. It's a bonus that my own grands are now a part of this, but we were doing it long before they were born. There are many ways to become involved in the lives of young people besides opening your home to them. You could teach a class, coach a sports team, or volunteer at a boys' or girls' club. If you don't have time for any of those activities, just invite your grandkids and a few of their friends over to watch a movie and share a meal. You'll be doing everyone involved a favor.

Don't Think in Stereotypes

Over the years, we boomers have prided ourselves in thinking outside the box, but often we fall into old-age stereotypical thinking anyway. We need to go back to our rebellious roots and forget about stereotypes that tell us what we should do or wear or where we should go. If you want to go see Ed Sheeran, go see him. I did and was thrilled that the audience was full of all ages, young and old. If you want to take a dance class, do it. (I added that last year. I'm not very good, but it sure is fun!) If you want to have long hair, let it grow. Those days of hairdos appropriate for ladies over fifty are gone. One of my good friends, Kim, who at fifty-something still has very long hair, recently took to Facebook to survey her friends. She titled the survey "Do It or You're Nuts, Don't Do It!" Her question was concerning whether she should cut her hair or keep it long. The responses she received were hilarious:

- "It's your hair."
- "Try something new."
- "No! I love your hair!"
- "I would be very careful if I were you."
- "It will grow back. DO IT!"

These are just a few of the many opinions her friends had. But no one said, "You're too old for long hair." I'm so happy the length of a woman's hair isn't determined by her age. I'm pretty sure it was at one point, because none of my mom's friends had long hair when I was growing up, and certainly no one had a grandma with long hair. Whatever you choose to do, just don't let being old stop you from being you!

Saying you're old is a self-fulfilling prophecy. Don't buy into it! My older sister was teaching a class recently that my mother was attending. When my sister referred to herself as old, my mother spoke up and said, "What do you think I am?" Everyone laughed, but Mom was making the point that my sister shouldn't refer to herself as old if someone in her audience is twenty years older. She made her point! Stay away from words like *old, feeble,* and *worn-out.* Focus on words like *youthful, energetic,* and *full of life.*

Keep Up with Current Affairs

Listening to the news can be pretty depressing, but staying current has a lot to do with staying young. While I don't like to dwell on the news, I make sure I listen to at least a few minutes a day. I do the same with sports, movies, and TV shows. I don't dismiss them as unimportant. Current events and new movies and TV shows are part of a young world, and in order for me to talk to the young people in my life, I need to stay current with what's happening in those areas. One of the reasons my grandkids don't consider me old is because I know who Lecrae is. If you don't, google him. Here's another one: What's Poshmark? Look it up. If you want to stay young, stay informed.

Resist Help with Mobility

This might just be me, but resist someone coming to your aid when you're getting up from a chair or opening a jar or stepping up a step. Until it's absolutely essential, don't depend on others to do what your body can still do. When my children were little, I made a pact with myself that I would not do things for them that they could do for themselves. Once they learned to tie their shoes, it was their job to tie their shoes. (Except those times when I was in crazy-momma busy mode and trying to get everyone out the door for church. Then I probably broke my pact, tied the shoes, and rushed them out the door.) In doing this, I was teaching my kids that I trusted them to do the things I taught them to do and was allowing them to grow to the next stage of life. I'm now applying that rule to myself, and I have for years. I never use an electric can opener if I have time to use the handheld one. It's just one more way for my muscles to work. I walk to the neighbor's house (which is Korie's or my mom's or my brother's house) instead of using the golf cart. I'm keeping my legs working. I carry in my own groceries. Again, chock it up to exercise. Okay, maybe I took this too far the last ski trip when I insisted on carrying my skies up the mountain to the chairlift, but you get the point. Once we stop doing things that challenge our muscles, we will start aging faster. My husband is the same. Our driveway is fairly long, but he always walks to check the mail. He lives by his Fitbit, making sure he gets in his ten thousand steps as many days as possible. It's true that I had to ban him from the attic after he fell through a few years ago, but for the most part, he keeps his body moving.

Remember, muscle memory disappears quickly. In the past, I have broken my kneecap and split a tendon in my ankle. I know what lack of exercise can do to a body as it recovers from an injury or illness. It's easy to become dependent on help while recovering, but doing what it takes to regain muscle strength will help you feel better about life in general.

Make Better Food Choices

"Okay, here she goes," you say. A skinny person telling us to eat better. Sorry, folks, but eating better is the key to maintaining a healthy weight and avoiding many health problems. I won't try to tell you to stick to any particular diet, because that is not my expertise, but I do know that studies have linked a typical American diet with many health risks. Unfortunately, the typical American diet includes many processed foods and sugary snacks. Over the years, my family has been guilty of not eating healthily. I made my share of packaged turkey sandwiches and went through way too many drive-in windows when my kids were growing up. I would like to use poor education as my excuse. It's a little like watching an old movie and seeing the movie stars smoking cigarettes. "That's crazy," we say—now. But not then. It was normal. We weren't aware of its many dangers to our health.

It's the same way with all that unhealthy food I fed my kiddos (sorry, kids). We didn't know that smoking was dangerous, and we didn't know that processed foods were unhealthy. The good news is that many of the bad effects of unhealthy eating can easily be turned around by simply eating healthier. Making better food choices for just a few weeks can result in more energy, better mental clarity, and the loss of unnecessary weight that can be robbing you of feeling young and more energetic. I like to think of eating healthy foods in terms of *what I can eat*, not *what I can't eat*.

Since Johnny's diagnosis of colon cancer, we have elected not to eat meat. Many people eat meat and do fine, but Johnny was convicted that meat contributed to his getting colon cancer. We both stopped eating it. Because we don't eat meat, the kids often say when picking a restaurant, "I forgot—you can't eat that." Then I gently remind them that we can; we just choose not to. This is true for any of us. God gives us the freedom to eat anything we want to eat, but that doesn't mean it's good for us to eat it. Remember 1 Corinthians 10, which says everything is permissible but everything isn't beneficial (see verse 23)? This is such a great way to look at the food we have available to us today.

Fortunately, we live in a very blessed nation. We have many choices—too many—of different kinds of foods. I've traveled to many countries where food choices do not exist. Countries where rice and beans are served every day for every meal. I've seen babies and adults who do not get enough of the necessary vitamins, and their health suffers for it. But we live in America, where food is plentiful for most of us. We need to remember that because it's plentiful, we have to be more responsible. In many ways, life is simpler with fewer choices, like for my sweet friends in the Dominican Republic, who never ask what's for dinner. They don't ask because it never changes. I'm thankful I live where choices are a possibility, but it causes me to have to choose wisely.

Another scripture comes to mind: Luke 12:48. It basically says that when much is given, much is expected. I know this verse wasn't intended to be a part of a diet discussion, but why not? In any area of life, when we are entrusted with much, we should be expected to handle it with wisdom and not take advantage of what is given to us.

I'll end this section by telling you that eating better really isn't hard. Here are the things to remember: limit or eliminate processed foods and sugary snacks and add more fish, vegetables, grains, and fruits. This is how we look at it: if it swims or grows, we eat it. One more thing: we're not perfect at this. You might see us eat a cupcake at a birthday party or run through the drive-through at a fast-food restaurant (but no hamburgers) on a busy day. Hey! You gotta live, right? But we try to choose the healthiest thing available for most of each day. I've heard health food experts call it the 80/20 rule. Eat healthy 80 percent of the time, and leave 20 percent for the extras. That might work for you. There is more than one way to skin a cat, as my dad used to say.

★ ★ ★ ★

Rockstar GRANDPARENTING

Stay away from words like *old*, *feeble*, and *worn-out*. Focus on words like *youthful*, *energetic*, and *full of life*.

Keep Working

Many look forward to retirement, only to discover that retirement leaves them bored and unfulfilled. Those I have interviewed tell me they miss having a purpose and having people in their lives to interact with. I don't believe staying at a job that is stressful and unfulfilling is the answer, but it's worth it to find a job, whether a volunteer or paid position, that excites you and makes you want to get up each day. Many studies point to the benefits of rewarding work in our later years, stating it may result in a longer life. I would say even if a longer life isn't the outcome, a life that is more satisfying is certainly worth it. For those of us in an active church, there is never a shortage of jobs to do. In fact, in many churches, if you just put your name out there, you'll never have a free day again!

Some Final Thoughts

Because I will be sixty-five when this book comes out (yikes!), I decided to make a list of statements that scream *old*. You might be old if . . .

- You groan when you get out of a chair or the car or the church pew or when moving in any direction at any time.
- You start most sentences with these words: "When I was your age . . ."
- You pick the comfy shoe with the stiff sole over the cute heels with a bow.
- Your pillbox is bigger than your old cassette tape case in the attic.
- You say no to going to any concert, even if it is Paul McCartney or Neil Diamond, stating, "It's too loud."
- Speaking of loud music—your hearing is worse, but the music always seems too loud.
- You pick restaurants by how quiet they are. (Guilty!)
- You insist that the old days were better, even if the old days included stoned friends and super loud music.
- You notice people offer you their seats on public transportation. (Or you are on public transportation and you don't live in New York.)

- If you're a lady, you get a short haircut; if you're a man, you let yours grow out, along with the hair in your nose and ears.
- You notice your grandkids or spouse saying, "You just told me that."
- When you get to the grocery store, you don't remember what you needed.
- You wear house slippers all the time, especially if you're a guy.
- You don't know who Jay-Z is and you don't care.
- Christmas decorating involves one tree on a table in the living room.
- You enjoy gardening, soft music, and *Antiques Roadshow.*
- You have misplaced all five pairs of reading glasses.
- You have a coat or sweater with you at all times "just in case."
- You listen to music only from your era. (Good thing ours was the best.)

—————

Gray hair is a crown of glory;
it is gained by living a godly life.

—Proverbs 16:31

How Sweet It Is

arvin Gaye released this song in 1964, but it was the James
Taylor version I loved to belt out as I cruised the roads with
two babies in tow. One baby sat in my lap, and the other one stood right
beside me with my "free" arm protecting her from possible injury. It's a
miracle any of us survived our youth, when sleeping in the back window of a car was prime car-ride territory. My children were in middle
school, or junior high as we used to call it, before the law required us to
do what common sense should have told us to do—wear seat belts. But
social situations change, don't they? We become better educated or en-
lightened about a belief or way of life, and all of a sudden, what we used
to do becomes nearly barbaric to our new way of thinking.

The first verse of this song starts with these words: "I needed the
shelter of someone's arms, and there you were."[1] These are powerful
words that declare what it means to depend on the love of someone and
to trust him with your ups and downs. I'm quite sure it was written for
a girlfriend, but now, as a grandmother, this song cries out to me as a
description of a loving, God-fearing family.

Besides commonsense issues, such as wearing seat belts, not smoking cigarettes, and slathering on sunscreen, people have come to realize

that many other social issues needed to be changed. One of these areas is adoption. Adoption is all about a child needing someone to call her own—a family she can trust to be there for her, through good times and bad. The child being adopted is in need, and the family blessed to adopt is in need. From the earliest days, adoption was an essential part of life in any community. Wars, illness, and unlawful behavior left children without families to raise them. So adoption, or the raising of someone else's child, is not a new concept, but it has developed socially, as other issues have.

Adoption entered our family many years ago when it wasn't fashionable or socially accepted to adopt. Johnny's family was well respected in their community. His dad was a leader in the church and a loving, supportive father to his children. When Johnny's sister Mary was still in high school, she became pregnant. Because Johnny's mother had a mental illness, Mary and her dad felt as if they had no choice but to put the baby up for adoption. A year after the baby was born and given a new home with two parents who loved him, Mary and Mac (the father of the baby), decided to get married. Mary and Mac struggled during the first few years of their marriage, but in their twenties, they rededicated their lives to Jesus and have been strong warriors for the Lord ever since. Their story is written in their book titled *Never Let Go*. They tell of God's protection over them and their son until, at nineteen, he reentered their lives. They also verbally share their story over and over again in an attempt to help others dealing with life issues find hope and comfort. As a family, this was a difficult journey for us to walk through.

When Mary discovered she was pregnant, it was decided she would go away to have the baby. No one in our community knew of her pregnancy, but through a series of events, Johnny and I found out. Behind the scenes, we did what we could to show our love and support to Mary both while she was away and after she came home. Eventually we all went back to our normal lives and only occasionally spoke openly of the event that was hidden deep in our hearts.

Twelve years later, I was asked to speak at a youth rally in Lafayette, Louisiana. I was thrilled to have the opportunity and excited to go to a youth event with my new teenager, Korie, who was fourteen at the time. We rode the church bus filled with happy teenagers to south Louisiana and arrived safely, pleased to meet our host family for the weekend. Host families are generally members of the church hosting the event, and attendees stay with these families. I was told there were no more homes available in Lafayette, but a family in a neighboring town had offered their house to us for the weekend. Of course, that was fine with us. We got in the car with this sweet couple, and I immediately felt strange about my surroundings. It was a feeling I couldn't explain. My default in strange situations is to talk, so I began to ask about their family. I was told they had only one son. It was after I asked what their son's name was that the hair on my arms stood up! "His name is Heath," the momma said, "and he is twelve years old."

Let me step back a bit. I didn't have much information about Mary and Mac's son. The adoption was twelve years earlier, and all the details were hazy. We didn't know where he lived or who adopted him, but we did know one thing: his name was Heath. In the entire state of Louisiana, was it possible that this was "our" Heath's family? My heart was racing as I asked one more question that would give it away. "When is his birthday?" I asked. I could justify asking because I had already told them I also had a twelve-year-old son. I sat in the back seat of that car, barely breathing as I waited for the response. "August 17," I was told. And then I knew. It was "our" Heath! The ride from Lafayette to their home in New Iberia couldn't have gone any slower. I couldn't wait to walk through their door. Even though they had told me he wasn't at home, I was eager to verify that it was truly him by looking at his pictures.

When we arrived at their home, I tried as hard as I could not to stare at the many pictures that covered their walls and tabletops. Pictures of a curly-headed boy who was, without a doubt, our Heath. I'm sure I was grinning from ear to ear. Then reality hit me. He wasn't *our* Heath; he was *their* Heath. I couldn't let them know who I was. I listened as Heath's parents shared with us their life journey with their son. They bragged on him. They smiled when they mentioned his name. They laughed as they told of his personality and witty side. On the outside, I was calmly listening and attentive to their words, but I had a party going on inside me. What a gift God gave our family that weekend! This was long before cell phones. Oh, how I would have loved having a phone with a camera to bring home precious photos of Heath to Mary and Mac. But they had to settle for one picture of the back of his head taken from a distance during the youth rally. I was too nervous to get my camera out and start snapping pictures. I did what I could.

Late in the night, after everyone was in bed, I remember sneaking into the kitchen to the phone that hung on the wall. (Remember those?) I called Mary and Mac collect, hoping the call wouldn't show up on the family's phone bill. I had to tell them where I was. When Mary answered, I said, "Mary, you won't believe where I am." "Where?" she asked. "I'm in Heath's house!" I frantically answered. "Why are in you in Mr. Heath's house?" was her reply. You see, we had a church member with the last name of Heath, and that's all she could think about. My being in her son's house wasn't even a thought! "No," I said, "I'm in your son Heath's house!" Then the screaming began as I told her the whole story of how I ended up at Heath's house.

That weekend event was all the confirmation I will ever need to let me know that God loves His children. He orchestrated every detail of that weekend and allowed me the gift of seeing Heath. Keep in mind, Johnny and I were the only family members, aside from Johnny's dad, who knew about his birth. I was the only one who would have been able to give Mary and Mac a report on their son. Anyone else chosen to stay in that home on that weekend would have had no idea about Heath. God used me in a mighty way.

I had no idea that adoption would play out in our family in other amazing ways in the future. When Korie was in high school, she admired one of the Bible teachers at the Christian school she attended. He and his wife had adopted a son, whom they named Charlie. From the day she heard about their son, Korie determined to adopt if God allowed her the opportunity. Korie had been a part of Heath's story too. Since she was with me at the youth rally, I felt I had to tell her why I was nervous and excited. I'm sure I was acting strange. At fourteen, she was understandably shocked to hear about her aunt and uncle's secret life. But she handled it like a champion and agreed to never tell anyone until Mary and Mac were ready to tell.

It was a heavy burden for a young teen, but she was up to the challenge. (Soon after this, Mary and Mac confessed to our church family, which resulted in changed lives for hundreds of others. Go on Amazon and order their book if you want to read more of their story.) Back to little Charlie. Korie loved it when little Charlie came to school, and from the example of this young Christian couple, she was able to see a family raising their own biological children as well as their adopted son. She also remembered the love she saw toward Heath from his adoptive parents. Korie's path to adoption was set in motion in the late eighties, but it would be a few more years before it came to life.

It wasn't until 2001 that God gifted us through adoption with our grandson Will. Korie and Willie already had two children, John Luke and Sadie, but Korie couldn't get the story of Charlie out of her mind. She had mentioned to others about the possibility of adopting, and apparently word had gotten to the right people. One day she and Willie got a phone call about a baby boy who needed a family. That was all it took. We all traveled to Baton Rouge to claim him as our own. When we got home, our church family had a huge shower for Korie to welcome five-week-old Will into our church family as well as our physical family.

If you follow Korie and Willie's story, you know they welcomed our Taiwanese granddaughter, Rebecca, into their family in 2005. Although Rebecca isn't adopted by law, she is adopted by love and is a part of our family as if the legal papers were signed. Korie and Willie opened their home again in 2014 when they adopted twelve-year-old Rowdy.

The adoption cycle in our family is complete, as we have experienced adoption from all angles. From Mary and Mac's journey, we lived through the agony of having to give a much-loved child to another family and totally trust them with his upbringing. From Korie's family, we have experienced the joy of being given not one but three children to love and raise as our own.

Praise God that adoption in America has evolved and there's more to adoption than the little cartoon story of Annie that many of us grew up reading and even laughing at. When I was young, besides that comic strip, adoption was seldom spoken about. If there was a child in my school who was adopted, I would have heard about it only in a whisper, as if it were a secret not to be shared with others. I don't know whether it was because most babies who were adopted came from teens who were unmarried and that stigma alone was enough to taint the whole process or whether it was a way of respecting the privacy of the child and family involved. In any case, adoption was never boldly celebrated with a party as it is today.

History tells us that adoption has always been a part of society. In fact, adoptions date back to biblical days. We know that Moses was adopted. Remember his trip down the Nile River? The Bible account in Exodus 2 says Moses's mother could no longer hide him from Pharaoh's men, who were instructed by decree to kill the baby boys born during this time. So with a heavy heart, she sent him down the river with the hope that someone would find him and love and care for him. As the story goes, Moses was chosen and adopted by Pharaoh's daughter.

As I became an adult in the 1970s, there was still some stigma attached to adoption. Even though the number of adoptions in America was steadily increasing with overseas adoptions, the fate of a young woman who found herself pregnant was yet to be handled in the best way. Society viewed this situation as one in which the mother made a terrible mistake and could not possibly successfully raise a child on her own. There were two choices: adoption or abortion. Mary and Mac would never consider abortion, leaving adoption as their only choice. Mary, like the mother of Moses, sent her baby off with a heavy heart, trusting that someone else would love and care for him as much as she would have, had she been able to keep him.

I've learned many lessons from the adoption stories in our family. I've learned that no matter how a baby enters a family, it is a sweet moment. Over the years, we have welcomed into our home unwed mothers, foster children, young couples who needed a place to land for a few months, older couples who were building a new house, single men and women who were not ready to live on their own, and people in many other situations. The number of people who have stayed in our home for more than six weeks now totals over eighty. But we never adopted a child. With Will's adoption, we became adoptive grandparents. Many of you are also grandparents of adopted children. Some of you might be looking forward to an adoption in your future, and perhaps you have some questions. We did. I think the questions facing adoptive grandparents are the same questions the parents might be asking. Will I love this child as much as I love the biological grandchildren? Will I be able to accept this child who doesn't look anything like me or my children? What if he has problems? What do we say to people who comment that she looks different from the other children?

When Korie started talking about adopting Will, we considered those questions for a few minutes and then decided the only question that mattered was whether we could love him. The answer to that question was yes, and because it was yes, no other question mattered. Oh, it matters that we have answers ready when comments are made, because they will be, but those answers don't affect our love for our grandchild. We discovered that color doesn't matter, size doesn't matter, shape doesn't matter; the only thing that matters is our decision to love. And that is true whether a child is biological or adopted. Love doesn't come from a gene pool; love comes from a God pool. Because of God's love and acceptance of us as His adopted children, we can love and accept all children into our family, no matter how they come to us.

Today's world also brings another reality—divorce and stepchildren. Once again, the question arises: Can I love these children as I love my other grandchildren? Of course the answer is yes, you can. But it's more complicated than adoption because they have another family who loves and supports them. In our case, Ashley's bonus kids live in another state where their mother's family lives. We do not get to see them very often. Our job, as bonus grandparents, is to just be there when we can or when they need us. We send birthday and Christmas gifts to them to let them know we love them and are thinking of them. We include them in our grandkid pics around the house. We try to spend vacation time with them in the summer, but if it conflicts with their other family, we understand that it doesn't mean they don't love us. Being an adoptive grandparent or a bonus grandparent or a biological grandparent isn't about us; it's about making a child feel loved and connected to a family. And the more family support, the better for the child. No one has ever been overloved! It's not possible to love a child too much.

One of my favorite grandchildren stories comes from our Maddox. He's the seventh in my lineup of grands, so finding his place might have been challenging to him. It wasn't challenging at all to me. If I had a hundred, I would love them equally. All my grandboys used to love to spend the night with me. They took over the comfy couch in the game room.

One evening my daughter Ashley was trying to get her three little ones gathered up to go home when she found Maddox lying on the couch, declaring he wanted to spend the night. She asked him why he loved to sleep on 2-mama's couch. His answer was priceless. He said, "I know when I fall asleep, someone will put a blanket on me." I love that! It defines what grandparents should do and be for their grandchildren.

Grandchildren should always feel as if their grandparents are there with a warm blanket to cover them up. Literally and figuratively. Grandparents have the opportunity to offer what no other person in a child's life can offer. They have a bond that, whether by blood or blessing, tells a child, "You belong." Belonging is a key component to feeling happy in life. Don't get confused here. I always vote for holy over happy, but feeling happy is important too. Belonging gives a sense of security that leads to a feeling of happiness.

From the beginning of time when God saw that it wasn't good for Adam to be alone, we learn that God values belonging, which leads to happiness. Throughout life, we search for belonging by joining groups such as chorus or band or the PTA or the Kiwanis club or a small group within our church family. These are all great connections that can bring meaning and purpose to our lives. But in any scenario, especially for kids, there is the possibility of disappointment and rejection. That's when family can step in and pick up the pieces of a broken heart. That's when a warm blanket can feel awfully nice and a hug can briefly take away the pain.

Giving your grandchildren that sense of belonging and love does many things for them. Here are just a few.

It Builds Self-Respect

I have never liked the word *self-esteem*. In fact, if you ask my mom about that word, she is quick to say it didn't even exist when she was being raised or raising us. (It's a new word, possibly given to us by the same community that supports explaining everything to your kids.) The Bible doesn't support the word *self-esteem*. Look at Romans 12:3: "Do not think of yourself more highly than you ought" (NIV). I like the word *self-respect* better. There are many verses that tell us we can be bold about who we are because God has created us for a purpose. In 2 Corinthians 10:17, we are told to boast in the Lord; in Isaiah 43:4, we are told we are precious in God's eyes; in Romans 5:8, we are told we were loved even when we were sinners; in Ephesians 2:10, we are told we are created for God's work. Unconditionally loving your grandchildren shows them what God's love looks like. To them, it's like watching God with skin on.

It Builds Self-Confidence

Children who experience love in their lives have a better sense of who they are. They approach the world with more confidence, giving them an army in their heads to defeat the negativity in the world today. I have no doubt that our granddaughter Sadie has been able to gracefully wade through the negativity that comes from being in the spotlight because of the strong family support she has been given. Life is going to rock the worlds of our grandchildren. Disappointments are a part of growing up, and we don't want to shield them from those learning experiences, but we do want to be available to help them through them.

It Teaches Them to Love Others

Feeling loved and knowing you are loved are not necessarily the same thing. My two grandmothers were very different. One of them rarely *showed* love. She wasn't touchy-feely. She didn't give gifts. She never attended our school functions. Did she love me? Yes, of course. I, and the other twenty-four of her grandchildren, knew we were loved. How did we know that? Basically, the only way we knew that was because she was our grandma and grandmas love their grandchildren. Oh yeah, there was the fact that she always asked for school pictures and kept them in her purse to show others. And I forgot—she was always up for a game of Scrabble. And then there were the times she played the piano for everyone to enjoy. You see, how children *perceive* showing love isn't always what love is. It is up to us as grandparents to teach children that loving doesn't always look the same. It's not about buying the latest video game or being in the front row at Grandparents Day or even staying home with a sick child. It's true, *love* is an action word, but there are many ways to act out love. Oftentimes love means not buying that video game but instead talking to your grands about delayed gratification. Love

Rockstar
GRANDPARENTING

Unconditionally loving your grandchildren shows them what God's love looks like. To them, it's like watching God with skin on.

might also mean telling your grands that Grandma has to work and can't make it to the event they are asking you to attend. The point here is that we have to help our grands understand that love is about support, sacrifice, communication, and a spirit of deep emotion, and not *things*. Things don't define love. They can represent love, as a wedding ring does, but they are not love. Love requires time and patience, and it always wants the best for the person loved.

For many years now, Korie and Willie have attended a hunting conference out of town, and their kids stay with me. I've always wanted to see what the conference is like, but keeping the kids, especially when they were little, was more important. Life clicked along and the kids got older. Plans were made for me to go to the convention, and a sitter was lined up to watch the kids. Two days before the trip, John Luke and Bella (ages sixteen and nine at the time) came down with the flu. There was no way I was going to leave them with anyone else. My trip was canceled, and I planned for a week at home nursing sick kids. On the third day, as the sickies began to feel better, I was back working in my home office. Around lunchtime, I stopped to fix everyone some lunch. To my surprise, on the kitchen counter was a bouquet of flowers made out of pipe cleaners and a note that read,

> We made this to show you that we thank you for taking care
> of us and helping us while we are sick. We love you. Thank you.
> John Luke Robertson and Bella

Yes, my heart melted. (How sweet it was!) I love how John Luke felt he should include his last name. Yes, I had to give up a fun trip, but knowing that my grandkids trust that I am there for them will always outweigh the fun I might have had.

John Luke is now grown, married, and away at college. I couldn't be happier for him, but if I sit behind a twentysomething young man in a baseball cap with long curly hair, I promise I may cry thinking about him. Many people think a family is made up of different personalities that do their very best at liking (loving is a given; liking is a challenge) one another in spite of those differences. But the Bible doesn't ask us to simply tolerate our family members; the Bible tells us to love, and that requires more work on everyone's part. I love the adult John Luke as much as I loved the little John Luke. My role in his life is different now, but the feelings are the same.

Yes, no matter how children come to us, our response should be the same—make them feel loved. I have a picture that was taken when we brought our firstborn, Korie, home from the hospital. In it, at least ten sets of hands are trying to touch her. That's how every child, every person, should feel—that he is loved by everyone in his life. Everyone should be able to say, "How sweet it is to be loved by you."

Above all, clothe yourselves with love, which binds us all together in perfect harmony.

—Colossians 3:14

Put Your Hand in the Hand

I started this book with a song whose lyrics come directly from the Bible. It seemed appropriate to end my book with this song sung by Anne Murray, Elvis Presley, Joan Baez, and even Bing Crosby. It was written by Gene MacLellan. My personal favorite recording is by Anne Murray. What a voice! As a teen, I would try to mimic that deep, rich sound of hers, but no matter how deep I went, my warbling sounded more like a squeaky mouse than Anne Murray's roaring lion. Oh well, God gifts us all in different ways, right?

I don't know why this song rose to the top of the charts in the early '70s except to say people needed Jesus then just as they need Him now. Many of the problems affecting our country today could be fixed if we all lived according to Scripture, as well as the words from another song by the Youngbloods that baby boomers cried out in the '60s and '70s: "Try to love one another." There were so many songs written with this message, yet as a human race, we can't seem to make it happen.

I dug out my yearbook from my senior year in 1971, and sure enough, "Everybody get together" was the theme for our annual that year. It was our battle cry! We desperately wanted the world to live in peace and harmony. Do you remember the opening line of that particular song, "Get Together"? The first line compares love to a song we sing.[1] Sadly, many of us, as we have gotten older, are more apt to believe that love *is* just a song we sing.

As the years pass, life can suck the fun and fantasy out of the adventure we dreamed we were going to live. Job disappointments, life-threatening illnesses, bitter divorces, deaths of friends and family members, and a list of other sad events are a far cry from the days of driving through the new McDonald's in our Volkswagen Beetle packed with the friends we thought we would have forever. On top of our own family experiences, listening to the news every day for fifty-plus years is enough to make all of us consider commune living again (minus the crazies and the drugs). Locking ourselves away on a remote property and raising a garden sounds pretty good on many days. But that is not reality. In real life, things happen. Right? And we have to cope and care and comfort and control and keep it together for the next generation.

Back to our song of choice for this chapter.[2] It's reported that Gene MacLellan, the writer of "Put Your Hand," was a believer in Jesus, which the words of the song of course reveal, so I was sad to read that he committed suicide in 1995.[3] Yes, life gets hard, even for people who write the songs that make millions of folks think and act differently. For our family, we have found the only way to survive is by doing just what this song says and putting our hands in the hand of the One who stilled the waters and calmed the seas.

John 16:33 tells us that in this world, we will have trials. That is a promise—not one we love to read about, but still, a promise. Maybe *promise* isn't a good word here. How about a warning? That's a better word for it, right? God is warning us to be prepared because troubled times will come. Why does God tell us this? Why doesn't God just take away the possibility of trouble? Why do I talk to grandparents who are raising their grandchildren because their daughter is on drugs? Why do I listen to grandmothers cry and look for answers when they discover a grandchild is drinking and partying? Why do grandparents have to fight for their money when greedy grandchildren threaten to take it from them? The list could go on forever, and the answer will always be the same—God created humans with the ability to choose. That ability gives each of us the right to decide between good and evil. Sadly, most do not see the generational damage that can be done by one bad decision.

Recently I heard a grandmother talk about her grandson who is making bad choices. At the end of our conversation, she smiled and said, "But the story isn't over yet. I am not giving up." And she won't. She will cry, plead, pray, intervene, and do anything else she needs to do to help that child not have a life of misery, regret, and shame. That's what grandparents do. But in the end, we can't fix everything. Hearts will be broken, relationships will suffer, and lives will be damaged.

We often quote 1 Corinthians 10:13 when we are trying to help someone struggling through a hardship. That verse says, "The temptations in your life are no different from what others experience. And God is faithful. He will not allow the temptation to be more than you can stand. When you are tempted, he will show you a way out so that you can endure." This verse is not about struggling but about being tempted. It's a great verse, but it seems to me that it isn't one to quote when helping a friend through suffering. Paul was right: all of us will be tempted in the same way, over the same sinful things. I recently reread the book of Acts, and over and over again the people were warned about sexual immorality, yet we still see it happening and hurting families today. Fortunately, we have the end of that verse to bring us comfort. God promised to be with us to help us say no to temptations. The sinful behaviors God warned the Israelites about are the same behaviors that affect us today. And those behaviors leave a mess that can sometimes last for generations.

As for suffering, there are other verses that give us hope and comfort when troubled times come, when things that are out of our control cause great pain. Psalm 46:1 tells us that God is always with us. He's our helper in times of need. Philippians 4:13 tells us we can handle all things through Jesus Christ. Psalm 9:9 tells us God is a stronghold in times of need.

My father-in-law taught us about suffering on this earth. At twenty-six years old, one week after Johnny was born, his dad heard his new baby crying. He went to find out what was wrong and discovered that his wife—Mamaw Howard to all of us and Queenie to him—had suffered a mental breakdown. A new baby, a young wife, a job with a future—everything in Alton Howard's life was perfect until that awful morning when his life changed forever. Before his death, he wrote his life story down for his family. Here are his words to describe that moment: "There was no expression on her face. No movement, total silence; only the cry of the baby broke the stillness. I could not get her to speak one word. She seemed to be unaware that I was even there; [she was] just standing there quietly, pressing our son to her breast."

Mamaw Howard was never again the vibrant brown-eyed beauty

Alton had married a few years earlier. There would be years of hospital stays, medication, and therapy. But Alton never gave up loving his bride and serving his God. Again, from Alton's words written later in his life:

> The first thing one must learn is to come to the realization that life must be a walk of faith. Otherwise, you will be overcome in searching for all the "whys" and "how comes." We must learn that what we see is not the total picture but only the present moment. God has so willed it that faith can only grow in the soil of trust and dependence. Always demanding an answer to everything that may befall us leaves faith standing outside to wither and die. For beneath the winter clouds of snow and rain are the seeds of spring and summer flowers. The greater blessings and growth usually do not come immediately, but more often later. There must be watering time and growing seasons.

Such precious words from a man who lived over fifty years with no answers to why his wife was destined to a life of mental anguish. I don't have the answers to the whys either, but I do know that his Queenie, Mamie Jean Howard, affected thousands of people in spite of her mental illness. God had a place for her in His story because she and Alton were faithful to Him. Her home was a welcoming haven for visiting missionaries, newlyweds seeking advice, those disheartened with life, the mentally and physically ill, and her family who loved her. She kept Bible verses posted all over their home and would often read her favorite verse, Isaiah 41:10, out loud to anyone in the home: "Fear thou not; for I am with thee: be not dismayed; for I am thy God: I will strengthen thee; yea, I will help thee; yea, I will uphold thee with the right hand of *my* righteousness" (KJV).

I can still hear her sweet voice as she emphasized certain words to give the verse more meaning. I learned so much about pain and suffering from Papaw and Mamaw Howard. Mostly, I learned that God is right there with us in the pain. He's crying with us. He's holding our hands. He's singing over us to soothe and comfort us. I love 2 Corinthians 4:17, which says, "For our present troubles are small and won't last very long. Yet they produce for us a glory that vastly outweighs them and will last forever!" I know God was preparing Mamaw Howard for her heavenly home, but mostly, He was preparing all of us who knew her and were blessed by her tremendous faith in her heavenly Father for our heavenly home.

As we learned to patiently wait for Mamaw to think of the correct word, as we watched Mamaw being taken away to the hospital, as we witnessed her struggle to feel as if she was good enough, as we listened to her chants in the early morning hours when she should have been sleeping, we learned to lean on God and look to Him for our help and hope.

Later in her life, after Papaw had gone on to heaven, the symptoms from Mamaw's illness were managed in a better way through newer medications. We delighted in seeing her enjoy a game of dominoes, cook dinner for friends, and travel to see her sisters. These are a few of the simple things she struggled to do as a young woman but in her seventies and eighties could fully enjoy. In some ways, the end of her life was better than the beginning, except she didn't have Papaw to share it with.

This may be true for your life as well. I hope it is. My daddy always encouraged his children to finish strong in anything we did. How do we finish strong when the storms of life have knocked us down too many times? Even if you've had a great beginning and middle, how do you make the last quarter count? Let's look at some of the keywords of this chapter's song and discover the hidden—or not-so-hidden—tips for today's grandparents.

The One Who Calms the Seas

This is it! This is the only answer to the questions we've been asking. Jesus is "the way, the truth, and the life" (John 14:6). Once, Jesus was called on by His disciples, who suddenly found themselves in an overwhelming storm. These were experienced fishermen, so this storm had to be out of the ordinary. They didn't know what to do. That's how we felt when my husband was diagnosed with cancer, when our children went through their divorces, when our parents died, when we took Mamaw to the mental hospital, and on and on. When you are faced with a storm, all bearing is taken from you, and no matter how hard you try, you can't get your boat to level out.

One summer John Luke bought a new sailboat and wanted to sail it on the ocean while we were on vacation. The wind and waves picked up just as he and his cousin Reed got offshore about fifty yards. There we sat on the shore, watching his little boat toss and turn in the wind and waves. We were overwhelmed with fear but helpless to do anything. We could see them struggling to get the boat under control, but we couldn't help. Anytime we watch our children or grandchildren go through tough times, it's as if we are on the shore but not close enough to help.

The story of Jesus calming the seas is found in Mark 4. The Bible says a furious squall came up and nearly overtook the boat. The disciples feared for their lives. They knew that help was on the boat with them, but He wasn't helping. Some have speculated that Jesus slept as a way of teaching the men to have faith. Of course, Jesus could have done that. I don't know. Perhaps He was exhausted. I've been exhausted before. Verse 38 says Jesus found a cushion and slept on it. Remember those "find me a pillow and let me sleep" days when your kids were babies? Exhaustion takes over and you just have to sleep. The Bible says Jesus "sent away the multitude" (verse 36, KJV). Apparently He had lived through a busy day of teaching, counseling, and loving His followers. I looked up synonyms for the word *multitude,* and *hordes, masses, crowds,* and *scores* came up. It makes me tired just reading those words. In any case, the disciples were terrified, but Jesus was asleep.

If Jesus was looking to test their faith, hands down, they failed the test. They woke Jesus up, asking whether He cared about them at all or whether He was just going to let them drown. I don't know what they thought He would do about their state of affairs, but from their reaction, which verse 41 describes as "terrified," I'm guessing yelling "Be still!" and having the waves obey Him wasn't what they expected. Jesus looked at His panic-stricken disciples and asked, "Why are you afraid? Do you still have no faith?" (verse 40).

At that point, I can only imagine the looks they gave one another. Perhaps they did the blame game, as our grandkids do, pointing fingers at one another. "I was fine. It was him who was scared." It's always someone else's fault, right? Here's what I believe. I don't think they knew Jesus yet. They had watched Him and walked with Him and witnessed many things, but they still didn't truly know Him. Later in verse 41, after witnessing Jesus's mighty power, they asked one another, "Who is this man?" Clearly, they were still learning who He was.

In our doubts and weaknesses, perhaps we still don't know the God we serve. Jesus did a great thing for the disciples and for us in that story. He taught us that whether He is awake or asleep, if He is in the boat, we have nothing to fear. In asking the disciples why they were afraid, He was saying, "Don't you know that when you ride with Me, you're always going to be okay?" For those of us who believe in Jesus Christ as our Lord and Savior, we don't ever have to doubt that He is going to take care of us. Does that mean nothing bad will happen in our lives? No, Jesus was content to sleep and let the storm rage on. He wasn't saving them from going through the storm; He was protecting them while they went through it. The disciples would have been safe either way— had He calmed the storm or let it rage. It wouldn't have changed the fact that they were protected.

Reaching out and taking the hand of the One who can save you is the first step to calming the storms in life. I know the questions some have as they try to understand a God who can allow bad things to happen to good people. I don't understand all of it either, but I do know this: God can and does make good come from bad. He doesn't cause the bad; He causes the good. Joyce Meyer says Good Friday isn't good because good things happened on that day; good things happened *because* of that day. Not all your days will be good, but if you trust in God, He will deliver the good days.

John Luke and Reed eventually made it safely back to the shore that day at the beach, but it wasn't because their grandparents or parents were able to do anything about the situation. We couldn't. Our only defense was prayer. So we prayed. Once they were safely on the shore, we asked them what happened. They told us one of the ropes broke and they kept going around in circles. Isn't that like life too? We keep repeating the same mistakes—going around and around, not securing the very thing that could help us get straight. Once they were able to secure the rope, they were able to steer the boat to safety. I love that story. I didn't love it as I watched from the shoreline, but I love it now. It continues to teach me to hold on to the One who can help me sail smoothly through life.

Looking at Others

In James 1:22–25, a mirror is used to illustrate the importance of hearing and heeding God's Word. We're told that if we listen to God's Word and don't obey it, it's like looking in a mirror and walking away, forgetting what you've seen. Mirrors aren't new inventions. Looking at a reflection in the water probably dates back to Adam and Eve, and there's evidence of mirrors similar to the ones we use today from centuries ago. Even though the mirrors of ancient days are a far cry from my magnifying makeup mirror that lights up, the illustration used by James was clearly understood by those listening to his words. (Soapbox: Our teens today hold a mirror in their hands nearly all the time. I've seen my granddaughters use their phones to put on lipstick, fix their hair, and get something out of their teeth. As a teen, I looked in the mirror while I got ready for school. Then maybe I looked in the car mirror just before

I ran into school. After that, it was likely I didn't see what I looked like until after PE class. No wonder our kids have identity issues. They see themselves too much! End of soapbox.)

Back to our song. This line tells us to take a look at ourselves and we will look at others differently. How does that really work? Well, it works only if we look at ourselves honestly. I'm pretty sure my sweet husband is the only human being who doesn't look in a mirror right before he goes out the door to work or church or wherever. Women, do your men do this? It drives me crazy! For us women, looking in a mirror on the way out the door is a given. And when we look in the mirror, chances are we are going to rearrange something. It might be moving one tiny hair, but something will change. As grandparents, we've lived a long time, done a lot of things, seen a bunch, and probably said more than we should, yet it's easy for us to get judgmental about our in-laws or our children or our grandchildren or the world in general. If we would stop a minute and take that look at ourselves—I mean really look at ourselves—we might see that we have a few things out of place too. Instead of being critical, we would be caring. Instead of being judgmental, we would be gentle. Instead of being negative, we would be nice. Looking closely at who we are and, perhaps, where we came from will cause us to view others as people who aren't perfect either but are still working on it.

The Holy Book

I'm proud to say that it's been our grandchildren who have led 2-papa and me to read and study the Bible more. I'm blown away by their thirst for knowledge and their desire to read more of God's Word. When we were teens, we loved God and followed Him, but we weren't challenged to know Him as our kids know Him today. I believe we, as a religious community, have grown up in this area. We've all been challenged to read more. The Bible is full of all kinds of advice for better living. It is the instruction manual for everything. From relationships to temptations to making wiser decisions, the Bible is the go-to book that can really help. It's not too late. If you haven't been a reader, you can start today. And it doesn't matter where you start. Just open the book and dive in. If you are looking for an easy-to-follow plan, you can read one chapter of Proverbs a day. There are thirty-one of them. It works out perfectly for one month of Bible reading.

Down on My Knees

Our family believes in the power of prayer. We just do. If you saw any *Duck Dynasty* episodes, you saw the family pray before the meal in the closing scene. I hope you know by now that prayer was never scripted. It was a meal, and the Robertson family prays before a meal. Period. When the first show aired, no one in the family expected the reaction that one prayer brought on. Comments such as "My family has never prayed before a meal. Thank you for showing us how to do that" and "My five-year-old asked me if our family could pray like your family does." Wow! Nope. Didn't see that coming. The Robertsons were intent not on preaching a sermon but on showing what their life is like, and that life includes prayer. For them, that prayer scene wasn't an add-on to spice up the show; it was real life. In fact, when the producer said the cameras were rolling and Phil said, "Let's pray," the producers had no idea what was about to happen. After the prayer, the producers said, "Are you going to do that every time?" Phil said, "Yep." And that—from my humble, somewhat of an outsider's but a little biased view—opened the door to others feeling empowered to speak more publicly about their faith.

Prayer is a way to connect with the One who has the power to heal, save, comfort, restore, and love like no other. Just having prayer as an avenue of conversation, a way to talk out problems, voice concerns, and applaud joyful things, brings hope and comfort, but it's much more. Prayer changes lives because God hears those prayers and acts on them. John 3:16 declares His love for us: God loved us enough that He gave His only Son to die for us. If God loved us to that degree, it makes sense that He would want to hear our pleas for help and answer them according to His wisdom, that He would want to listen to our cries for comfort and cover us with His hand, that He would enjoy listening to our shouts of joy and thanksgiving.

When my children were little, we were watching TV one day when the mom on the show started crying. My son, Ryan, was only three at the time, but I remember this clearly. He looked at me and said, "Moms don't cry." Immediately it hit me that he had never seen me cry. In his little world, moms didn't cry. Then it hit me: What other things did he think moms don't do? Like praying. Up until that point, I had depended on my quiet time for major prayer time. But from that day on, I made sure I prayed in front of my children, not just at mealtimes but other times too. I made sure they saw me read my Bible and study God's Word. You see, it's easy for us to get busy with life and save our prayer and Bible study time for our quiet time, our alone time. And that's good too. But don't hide all your God moments from your children and grandchildren. They need to see them.

Recently I was taking Aslyn, one of my granddaughters, to take her driver's education test. She was very scared and nervous. As we drove down the road, she said, "Will you pray for me?" Absolutely! Why hadn't I thought of it myself? My only answer to that question was that I was driving, but still! I happily prayed (with eyes open) for God to give Aslyn everything she needed to stay calm and recall all the information she had diligently studied. My heart was overjoyed that Aslyn could trust me to pray for her and that she knows there is power in prayer. Aslyn wasn't the first of my grandchildren to ask me to pray during a difficult time, and I know she won't be the last. We are intentional about showing our grands that God is in charge of everything and nothing takes Him by surprise. Isaiah 55:8–9 says,

> "My thoughts are nothing like your thoughts," says the LORD.
> "And my ways are far beyond anything you could imagine.
> For just as the heavens are higher than the earth,
>   so my ways are higher than your ways
>   and my thoughts higher than your thoughts."

Teach your grands that God is completely in charge of everything that happens in His universe, even if we don't always understand what's going on. When our family has experienced its most difficult days, we've leaned in closer to the One who can get us through them. Recently Aevin, our youngest grandson, had a terrible bicycle accident. My son sent me the prayer Aevin prayed after he saw a doctor in the emergency room and received several stitches. He prayed, "Dear God, I never once doubted You." Wow! I'm so thankful Aevin can voice that confidence in God at thirteen years old.

So we pray. We pray before meals. We pray when someone is sick. We pray before we get in a plane or a train or a car. We pray when disaster hits our country. We pray when someone has a job interview. We pray before a big test or game or performance. We pray when good news is announced. We pray when bad news comes our way. We pray for all of it because we believe God works today.

Do What You Must Do

And finally, I love the end of this song. What or whom do you live for? I recently read a blog by a young lady who, at age twenty-seven, has been given the news that she has incurable cancer. She challenged her readers to think about how they would spend their days if they had only six months, a year, maybe two to live. A diagnosis like that changes everything, doesn't it? As grandparents, we know the brevity of life. We're not there yet, but we're nearing the end. In many ways I know I am preaching to the choir, telling you to value your days. But we all need reminders, right? I don't just want to remind you to value your days; I want to remind you to make them count.

The other day, I got a new cell phone. I was visiting with John Luke, holding my new phone in my hand, when someone called. I almost didn't answer it because the ringtone wasn't one I was used to. After I hung up, I told John Luke I would have to change my ringtone later. He took my phone, went to ringtones, tried a few, found my old one, and fixed it. It took him about a minute. His comment was "2-mama, if you can do it in one minute or less, do it now." (He had obviously been reading a new book on time management or happiness or something. He's our reader.) But the point was well taken. I started thinking about all the things we do that would require only one minute but we put them off until they become big things that take an hour or two or three. Here's a great example: When I was a young bride, I would put off washing two plates and two glasses until I had ten plates and ten glasses to wash. Without knowing it, over time I began to apply John Luke's wisdom, and for many years now, I haven't let dishes stack up. If I eat a bowl of cereal, I clean the bowl right then or put it in the dishwasher. Why didn't I do that as a young bride? Well, you don't know what you don't know, and I didn't know that little things become big things if they aren't taken care of. It was a lesson I had to learn.

After my conversation with John Luke, I began to think more about this principle and how we can apply it to our relationships. After all, as the line in the song says, our main purpose in life is to take care of our kids and our spouses. How can I apply the one-minute principle to my relationships? Certainly not everything can be done in one minute, but some things can. And when those good little things stack up, they can be life changing and life affirming for those we love. Here are a few one-minute things you can do to have a sink full of blessings:

1. Text a grandchild a heart emoji. It takes less than a minute, but it says "I love you" and "I'm thinking of you."
2. Before you go to work in the morning, write "I love you" on your spouse's mirror with a dry-erase marker.

3. If she lives nearby, run by your mother's house, hand her a flower, and give her a kiss.

4. Call a grandchild (or anyone) and say, "I have only one minute, but that minute is for you. Just wanted to tell you I'm thinking about you."

5. Send a picture that was taken during a fun time with a family member and say, "I loved this moment with you."

6. Pick up doughnuts on the way to work to share with coworkers. Write on the box, "Have an awesome day!"

7. Pick up lunch for your school-age grands. Write a quick note on the sack or box that will be sure to embarrass them. On the inside, they will love it.

8. Send a card to your grands. Old-fashioned mail is still fun to receive and takes only a minute.

9. Order flowers to be delivered to a grandchild who's about to perform or has a big test or just to say "I love you."

10. Send your grands in college a gift card for dinner out and say, "Enjoy! I love you."

I could go on and on with these ideas, but you know what to do. Take that principle of a little going a long way in building great relationships and run with it. One-minute yourself into a happy life!

One Last Thing

Have you heard the story of James J. Braddock? Maybe you saw the movie about his life called *Cinderella Man* or read the book by the same name. I'm going to summarize it as I end my book. James J. Braddock was a boxer in New York City who was forced to give up boxing after losing numerous matches and breaking his right hand. (Seriously, I never understood this sport, but my daddy loved it.) The Great Depression was in full swing in America, and work was hard to come by. Braddock found work as a laborer on the docks doing anything and everything so he could feed his family, but that work wasn't consistent. Many days he walked three miles to the docks of Weehawken and Hoboken to see whether work was available, only to discover the answer was no. From there, he walked two more miles to West New York. If the answer was no there, he looked for odd jobs, such as shoveling snow or serving in a bar. His young family was left cold and hungry, waiting for his return each day. After nine months of scraping and scrounging for any amount of money, he was picked to fight Corn Griffin. He hadn't fought or worked out in nine months, and everyone suspected it would be an easy win for Griffin. But Braddock pummeled Griffin. And from that fight on, he continued to win. His broken right hand had been his power hand, but unable to use it while working on the docks, Braddock had been forced to use his left hand, giving him power in both hands. James J. Braddock went on to fight and win the heavyweight championship title against Max Baer in 1935. Here's the point of this story. Stay with me. Later, his wife, Mae, was quoted as saying, "My husband wasn't seeing Max at all when he was in the ring fighting. What he saw was a fierce ogre, trying to keep him from chasing the big bad wolf from our door. He was thinking of me, and of the kids, every minute of those fifteen terrific fighting rounds."[4]

While boxing isn't my sport of choice, I love this story. I love how this wife knew why her husband was in that boxing ring. It wasn't because of the glory he would receive. It wasn't because he was angry and had to get it out. It wasn't because it was a sport he loved. Though all those things might have been true, Mae Braddock knew her husband was fighting for his family. He had experienced the pain of watching his children go hungry, and he said, "No more!"

It all comes down to this question: Who are you fighting for? Nothing saddens me more than hearing of people reaching old age and having no one to take care of them. My uncle was asked to care for an older man at church as he reached the end of his life. When my uncle questioned whether he had children and grandchildren, he was told he did but they didn't have a relationship. How sad for that man and his family. They let go of

Rockstar GRANDPARENTING

Grandparenting requires sacrifices of time and resources, but it will be worth it when our grandchildren launch their lives from the firm foundation we laid for them.

one of the most precious gifts God gave us—family. Discovering who you are fighting for will change the course of your life. It will change how and why you wake up every morning. It will challenge you to make different choices.

For me, my first fight is for God and His kingdom. Then I fight for my family and the legacy I want to leave them. Those two things, God and family, cause me to wake up in the morning energized and go to bed at night eager for the next day. Every morning I anticipate how God will use me that day, and if He doesn't show me something specific, I go to my plan B, which I'm quite confident is His plan A.

Grandparenting requires sacrifices of time and resources, but it will be worth it when our grandchildren launch their lives from the firm foundation we laid for them. So . . . keep loving, keep caring, keep hugging, keep comforting, keep encouraging, keep teaching, keep showing, and keep rocking until you can't anymore. And then you will walk through heaven's gates and hear these words: "Well done, my good and faithful servant" (Matthew 25:21).

Praise the Lord.
Blessed are those who fear the Lord,
   who find great delight in his commands.
Their children will be mighty in the land;
   the generation of the upright will be blessed.
Wealth and riches are in their houses,
   and their righteousness endures forever.

—Psalm 112:1–3, NIV

A Special Word for Grandparents Raising Grandchildren

I want to talk a little here to grandparents who are raising their grandchildren. Bless your heart if you are one of these amazing grandparents. The American Association for Marriage and Family Therapy said that "there are approximately 2.4 million grandparents raising 4.5 million children."[1] This is a staggering statistic and one that brings me sadness as I consider all the reasons children might be living with their grandparents instead of their moms and dads. Other statistics point to the many challenges both the children and the grandparents in this situation face. One factor is the difficulty that grandparents face in stepping back and thinking like parents again instead of grandparents. After all, grandparents are supposed to have all the joy but not much responsibility, right? We're supposed to be able to send them home. But if you find yourself in the driver's seat again, you can't send them home. You are in charge, and basically, it can stink on many levels.

If you have been given this challenge, it's probably because there are no other solutions. If that's the case, you have no choice but to rise up and be thankful you are there for your grandchildren. I recently met a couple who accepted the challenge and took in their twelve-year-old grandson after a bitter divorce. There were three children in this family, but this one was struggling the most. He was angry and defiant. This wasn't going to be an easy job. Still, these wonderful grandparents put aside their vision of "dream retirement"—traveling in a motor home to see their children—in order to stay home and parent a sad, belligerent middle schooler. They both beamed as they proudly told me he is graduating from high school this year with straight As and they are busy looking at colleges for him to attend. The grandpa said, "It was the best decision we ever made. We know we changed this boy's life. The life in the motor home would have been fun; this life made a difference."

One of my dearest friends found herself in this situation when her grandchildren were ten and eleven years old. All other means of intervention had not worked, and her grandchildren were in a very bad, even dangerous, situation. After much prayer and conversation, the children were taken from their home and placed with their grandparents. Raising two children when the luxury of an empty home and quiet nights was part of their lives wasn't easy, glamorous, or even fun on many days, but it was necessary. My friend and her husband did what they never dreamed they would have to do to invest in their grandkids. They eventually adopted both children, who are now in college, well adjusted, and forever thankful for the role their grandparents played in their lives.

Since I haven't been in this position, I can't tell you how to do it, but I can tell you what I learned from a friend I'll call Diana.

Be Honest

From the first day the children came to live with Diana, she was honest about their situation. She told them their mommy and daddy had made some poor decisions that resulted in them coming to live with her. This was hard for them to totally understand when they were young, and over the years, Diana found herself having to repeat what had happened. She always told them the facts and avoided turning the discussion into an emotional trauma fest. She was careful to not let the pain of the past events show. She wanted the kids to have a normal life, which meant she didn't want them to constantly think about their parents and what had happened. That meant not talking about it all the time but letting months go by until one of the kids wanted to know more. Then she honestly answered their questions.

Work on Stability

For any child, a stable life is a better life. Diana and her husband quickly put the kids in a school they trusted, helped them choose extracurricular activities they valued, and made sure they had a church family they could connect with. Once again, as grandparents, this wasn't where their lives had been for many years, but Diana knew for the sake of the children, they had to get back into it. They traded in quiet evenings at home for ball games, fund-raisers, summer camps, car pools, homework, counseling, and a house full of friends. It was indeed a trade-off but one they can say was worth it.

Seek Help When Needed

Going through anything traumatic will make waves bigger than your boat might be able to handle. Seeking help from professionals if you need it is an important piece of the puzzle. Not seeking help can also be beneficial. Diana was careful to watch for signs of struggle but also careful to note the struggles that were normal parts of growing up. She didn't become jumpy, thinking that everything that troubled the children had a direct link to their situation. Some things are struggles for kids just because they are kids. There were other things Diana knew the children might need help working through, so she found a therapist trained to help when those times came up. It does take wisdom and discernment to figure this out, but you can do it!

Keep First Things First

Putting your grandchildren's well-being over your own child's poor decisions is never easy, and this is always the case when grandchildren are removed from their parents' home. There will be letters, calls, emails, and texts that will be hurtful to you as the grandparent trying to do the right thing. I watched as my friend constantly looked for the truth in the situation and did what she knew was the right thing. She leaned on friends and family members to shoulder the hurt from these communications, and she shielded the children. She continually asked God for wisdom and guidance, and He gave it to her.

Rest in What You've Done

Just like parents raising their children, grandparents who raise their grandchildren worry and doubt that they are doing enough. The good news is that "good enough" really is good enough. We don't have to be perfect; we just have to be willing. As parents, we had to go to bed at night and rest, knowing we did all we knew to do with that day. Grandparents, you must do the same. When we become parents, it's generally by our choice. When you become a grandparent who takes on the responsibility of a parent, you didn't get to choose. It's a responsibility that came to you by the bad choices of another person. But once there, the job is the same. Do what you can do, and then turn the rest over to God.

The Howard Family Legacy of Principles for Living

1. Actions have consequences; you reap what you sow. Your actions affect others. "I am responsible."
2. Respect God.
3. Family is important; there should be mutual respect and consideration within the family.
4. Respect government. Salute the position, if not the person.
5. Respect your employer. Salute the position, if not the person.
6. Do your duty. Some things we must do, like it or not.
7. Have faith. Trust God no matter what happens.
8. Be reverent. Worship God with all your strength, mind, and soul.
9. You have significance. You are made in the image of God.
10. We all have opportunity and the potential to do great things (risk/reward concept).
11. Be content. Happiness should not depend on your circumstances. Let it come from within.
12. Be self-disciplined. You shouldn't have to be told to control yourself.

13. Have courage. God will always be there. Take godly risks. You must step out and try things that are good.

14. Be responsible—and respond properly to your responsibilities.

15. You are not an owner but a manager. Treat all possessions as such. Give the owner (God) a fair return on His investment.

16. It's better to have little and be in Jesus than to have much and lose eternal life.

17. Be flexible.

18. Keep your priorities straight. Make first things first.

19. Recognize individual differences and accept them. Be tolerant and patient.

20. Practice active listening.

21. Be a good sharer; confess your sins, your fears, and your victories.

22. Have a sense of humor and use it correctly. Don't make fun of others.

23. Be a balanced individual. Have a balanced life.

24. Be committed to God, family, and others.

25. Always have a positive attitude and a can-do spirit.

26. Have a good prayer life. It will help you through every problem.

27. Have a healthy lifestyle. Take care of your body. Eat right and get plenty of good exercise.

28. Have an urgency for the lost.

29. Never stop learning. Get a good education and study on your own for the rest of your life.

30. Practice what you preach.

31. Don't be selfish or self-indulgent.

32. Be considerate of others and their belongings. Respect their privacy.

33. Persevere. Never give up. Be diligent.

34. Never intentionally hurt people's feelings.

35. Remember that people are more important than things.

36. Be honest and truthful. Doing what is right is never wrong!

37. Be hospitable. Open your home to others.

38. Be benevolent. Help those less fortunate. Be willing to share anything you have. Be compassionate.

39. Focus on the eternal, not the temporary.

40. Don't be afraid to be different.

41. All you need is love; love your neighbor as yourself.

42. Be gentle.

43. Never forget what Jesus did, is doing, and will do for you.

44. Be merciful and forgiving.

45. Be humble.

46. Have the heart of a servant; think like one; act like one. Don't serve only when asked.

47. Be mindful of God's creation and respect it.

48. Guard your mind. Think pure thoughts.

49. Check all beliefs and principles against the Bible.

50. If you can't say something nice, don't say anything at all. Don't gossip. If you wouldn't say it to a person's face, don't say it at all.

51. Accept criticism and correction graciously, and use them to your advantage.

52. Handle guilt; don't let it handle you.

53. Don't be afraid to admit you are wrong.

54. Say you are sorry first.

55. Don't worry. Don't be anxious.

56. Don't keep records of wrong.

57. Let Jesus be your example. Be known as a follower of Christ. Be like Him. Always ask, "What would Jesus do?"

58. Pass this legacy on to your children and your children's children.

Acknowledgments

With special thanks to my maternal grandparents, Flemon Madison and Myrtle Anne Durham; my paternal grandparents, John Clifton and Lela Mae Shackelford; my parents, Betty Jo and Luther Neal Shackelford; and my in-laws, Alton Hardy and Mamie Jean Howard. Each of you, in your own way, were rockstar grandparents, even before rock began! You showered all your grandchildren with love and began a legacy of faith and family.

My sweet husband, John Howard. Thank you for always supporting my craziness and being the best 2-papa ever. I couldn't do all I do without you.

To Bruce Nygren and everyone at WaterBrook. Thank you for believing in my book and helping me bring it to life.

To my grandchildren. Thank you for letting me tell your stories; post Instagram pics; beg you to sing, dance, and act; and love you like crazy. You are rockstar grandkids!

Notes

Introduction

1. "The Beatles," The Ed Sullivan Show: The Official Ed Sullivan Site, www.edsullivan.com/artists/the-beatles.

2. Landon Y. Jones, *Great Expectations: America and the Baby Boom Generation* (New York: Ballantine, 1986), 10.

3. "Baby Boomers," History, www.history.com/topics/baby -boomers.

4. Hal M. Bundrick, "Boomers' Biggest Retirement Regret? They Didn't Work Longer," The Street, May 15, 2015, www.thestreet .com/story/13152984/1/boomers-biggest-retirement-regret-they -didnt-work-longer.html.

5. "Surprising Facts About Grandparents," Grandparents.com, www .grandparents.com/food-and-leisure/did-you-know/surprising -facts-about-grandparents.

6. The Beatles, "When I'm Sixty-Four," by Paul McCartney and John Lennon, *Sgt. Pepper's Lonely Hearts Club Band,* copyright © May 26, 1967, Capitol Records.

Chapter 1: Turn! Turn! Turn!

1. Paul Zollo, *Songwriters on Songwriting,* rev. ed. (Boston: Da Capo, 1997), 8.

2. "Answer: Turn," Dailyanswers.net, http://dailyanswers.net /opportunity-or-obligation-to-do-something-that-comes -successively-to-each-of-a-number-of-people.

Chapter 2: The Name Game

1. Dr. Seuss, *Oh, the Places You'll Go!* (New York: Random House, 1990), 44.

2. Lois Wyse, *Funny, You Don't Look like a Grandmother* (New York: Crown, 1989), 39.

Chapter 3: Help! I Need Somebody—Help!

1. Jean M. Twenge, *Generation Me: Why Today's Young Americans Are More Confident, Assertive, Entitled—and More Miserable Than Ever Before,* rev. ed. (New York: Atria, 2014).

2. Wikipedia, s.v. "Help! (Song)," last modified June 27, 2018, 16:08, https://en.wikipedia.org/wiki/Help! (song).

Chapter 4: A Hard Day's Night

1. The Beatles, "A Hard Day's Night," by Paul McCartney and John Lennon, *A Hard Day's Night,* copyright © July 13, 1964, Capitol Records.

2. "Life Expectancy for Social Security," Social Security Administration, www.ssa.gov/history/lifeexpect.html.

3. National Center for Health Statistics, *Health, United States, 2016: With Chartbook on Long-Term Trends in Health* (Hyattsville, MD: 2017), 115, www.cdc.gov/nchs/data/hus/hus16.pdf#014.

4. Alton Howard, *Money Grows on Trees: How to Make, Manage, and Master Money* (West Monroe, LA: Howard, 1991), 21.

5. Howard, *Money Grows on Trees,* xiv.

6. *Merriam-Webster,* s.v. "peace," accessed July 16, 2018, www.merriam-webster.com/dictionary/peace.

7. Dave Ramsey, "Everything You Need to Take Control of Your Money: Track Spending with Our Budgeting Tool," daveramsey .com, www.daveramsey.com/fpu?int_cmpgn=new_year _campaign_2018&int_dept=fpu_bu&int_lctn=Blog-Text _Link&int_fmt=text&int_dscpn=CTA_for_Debt_Snowball _blog_#in-progress=1.

8. Howard, *Money Grows on Trees,* 185–86.

9. Howard, *Money Grows on Trees,* 246.

Chapter 5: Teach Your Children

1. Crosby, Stills, Nash, and Young, "Teach Your Children," by Graham Nash, *Déjà Vu,* copyright © March 11, 1970, Atlantic Records.

Chapter 6: Sound of Silence

1. Marc Eliot, *Paul Simon: A Life* (Hoboken, NJ: Wiley, 2010), 40.

2. Simon & Garfunkel, "The Sound of Silence," by Paul Simon, *Wednesday Morning, 3 A.M.,* copyright © October 19, 1964, Columbia Records.

Chapter 7: Let It Be

1. The Beatles, "Let It Be," by Paul McCartney and John Lennon, *Let It Be,* copyright © May 8, 1970, Apple Records.

2. Stephen J. Spignesi and Michael Lewis, *100 Best Beatles Songs: A Passionate Fan's Guide* (New York: Black Dog & Leventhal, 2004), 303.

3. "Paul McCartney, "Paul McCartney: Musician," in *The Right Words at the Right Time,* ed. Marlo Thomas (New York: Atria, 2004), 217–18.

4. Rick Warren, *The Purpose Driven Life: What on Earth Am I Here For?* (Grand Rapids, MI: Zondervan, 2002), 275.

5. Whitney Houston, "One Moment in Time," by Albert Hammond and John Bettis, *1988 Summer Olympics Album: One Moment in Time,* copyright © 1988, Arista Records.

Chapter 8: Wish I Was a Kellogg's Cornflake

1. Simon & Garfunkel, "Punky's Dilemma," by Paul Simon, *Bookends,* copyright © April 3, 1968, Columbia Records.

Chapter 9: I Got You Babe

1. Sonny & Cher, "I Got You Babe," by Sonny Bono, *Look at Us,* copyright © 1965, Atco Records.

2. Sheri Stritof, "Estimated Median Age of First Marriage by Gender: 1890 to 2015," The Spruce, last modified April 4, 2018, www.thespruce.com/estimated-median-age-marriage -2303878.

3. The Turtles, "So Happy Together," by Alan Gordon and Garry Bonner, *Happy Together,* copyright © 1967, White Whale Records.

4. Paul Raj, C. S. Elizabeth, and P. Padmakumari, "Mental Health Through Forgiveness: Exploring the Roots and Benefits," *Cogent Psychology 3,* no. 1 (2016), https://doi.org/10.1080/23311908 .2016.1153817.

Chapter 10: Leader of the Pack

1. The Shangri-Las, "Leader of the Pack," by George Morton, Jeff Barry, and Ellie Greenwich, *Leader of the Pack,* copyright © 1965, Red Bird Records.
2. Erik H. Erikson and Joan M. Erikson, *The Life Cycle Completed,* rev. ed. (New York: Norton, 1998).
3. Jennifer Winters, "Ten Best-Mannered People of 2017," National League of Junior Cotillions, January 4, 2018, https://nljc.com /ten-best-mannered-people-of-2017.

Chapter 11: When I'm Sixty-Four

1. The Beatles, "When I'm Sixty-Four," by Paul McCartney and John Lennon, *Sgt. Pepper's Lonely Hearts Club Band,* copyright © May 26, 1967, Capitol Records.

Chapter 12: How Sweet It Is

1. James Taylor, "How Sweet It Is," by Brian Holland, Lamont Dozier, and Eddie Holland, *Gorilla,* copyright © May 1, 1975, Warner Bros. Records.

Chapter 13: Put Your Hand in the Hand

1. The Youngbloods, "Get Together," by Chet Powers, *The Youngbloods,* copyright © 1967, RCA Victor.
2. Anne Murray, "Put Your Hand in the Hand," by Gene MacLellan, *Honey, Wheat & Laughter,* copyright © 1970, Capitol Records.
3. Nick Talevski, *Knocking on Heaven's Door: Rock Obituaries* (London: Omnibus, 2006), 388–89.

4. "Under-Appreciated Fight Films," Art of Combat International, www.artofcombat.org/art-of-combat---viper-s-views-cinderella-1-15.html.

Appendix 1: A Special Word for Grandparents Raising Grandchildren

1. Megan L. Dolbin-MacNab and Ryan M. Traylor, "Grandparents Raising Grandchildren," American Association for Marriage and Family Therapy, www.aamft.org/Consumer_Updates/Grandparents_Raising_Grandchildren.aspx.

About the Author

Chrys Howard is the mother of Korie Robertson, reality TV star from A&E's *Duck Dynasty*. Chrys holds a degree in elementary education and spent ten years teaching children with learning differences. After teaching, she joined the family-owned business, Howard Publishing, now known as Howard Books, where she served as senior editor and creative director.

She has authored a number of books, with more than one million in print, including the best-selling *Hugs for Daughters* and *Motivationals for Mom*. She coauthored the *New York Times* bestseller *Miss Kay's Duck Commander Cookbook; Strong and Kind* with daughter Korie Robertson; the children's book *D Is for Duck Calls* with Kay Robertson; and *Live Original Devotional* with granddaughter Sadie Robertson.

Chrys has spent more than forty years working with Christian youth camps; speaking to women's groups; teaching Bible classes to children, teens, and young adults; and traveling overseas for mission efforts.

Chrys and her husband, John, have three children and a growing number of grands and their spouses, plus one great-grandchild. She lives in West Monroe, Louisiana—next door to daughter Korie and her husband, Willie—and is surrounded by other family members.